Multiple intelligences

....A thematic approach

body wise

bodily–kinaesthetic

word wise

verbal–linguistic

logic wise

logical–mathematical

people wise

interpersonal

nature wise

naturalist

music wise

musical–rhythmic

picture wise

visual–spatial

self wise

intrapersonal

Multiple intelligences *(Lower Primary)*

First published by R.I.C. Publications 2004

Reprinted under license by
Prim-Ed Publishing 2004

Copyright© R.I.C. Publications 2004

ISBN 1 920962 19 0

PR–0747

Additional titles available in this series:
Multiple intelligences *(Middle Primary)*
Multiple intelligences *(Upper Primary)*

Internet websites

In some cases, websites or specific URLs may be recommended. While these are checked and rechecked at the time of publication, the publisher has no control over any subsequent changes which may be made to webpages. It is *strongly* recommended that the class teacher checks *all* URLs before allowing children to access them.

View all pages online

http://www.prim-ed.com

Foreword

The theory of multiple intelligences places value on a range of eight different learning intelligences—acknowledging individual differences. Teachers and children favour a particular learning style (or styles). This series aims to provide teaching and learning opportunities, using the eight multiple intelligences through a thematic approach in the classroom.

Titles in this series:
Multiple intelligences – Lower Primary
Multiple intelligences – Middle Primary
Multiple intelligences – Upper Primary

Contents

Teachers notes

What is 'multiple intelligences'?

The theory of multiple intelligences was developed by psychologist Dr Howard Gardner after years of biological and cultural research into human cognition.

In his 1983 book, *Frames of mind: the theory of multiple intelligences*, Gardner suggests that there are seven (later eight) different types of human intelligence or ways of understanding the world—and possibly even more yet to be identified. This idea is in contrast to the traditional view of intelligence, where it is thought of as a general characteristic that affects our skills and abilities. IQ tests are a perfect example of this latter belief.

Gardner believes that each person has one or two dominant intelligences, although it is possible to strengthen all eight. He points out that our intelligences aren't used in isolation;

instead, one activity or task requires the use of a number of intelligences working together.

The eight intelligences identified by Gardner are verbal–linguistic, logical–mathematical, naturalist, visual–spatial, bodily–kinaesthetic, musical–rhythmic, interpersonal and intrapersonal. Typical characteristics of a child with a dominance in an intelligence and suitable activities for developing or assessing each intelligence are outlined below. Each of these intelligences is also described on the teacher page preceding each worksheet.

To make the terminology easier for the children to understand, the terms have been simplified with an accompanying icon for each intelligence.

Intelligence		Activities involving ...
Verbal–Linguistic A child who thinks in words. He/she learns best through activities involving reading, writing and speaking.		verbal and written communication, vocabulary, word puzzles and games, spelling, listening to people speak or read aloud
Logical–Mathematical A child who thinks rationally and in abstractions. He/she learns best through activities involving numbers and patterns.		problem-solving, brainteasers, logical puzzles, questioning how things work, science experiments, number games or problems, complex ideas
Naturalist A child with an awareness of the patterns in nature. He/she learns best through activities involving animals, plants and the environment.		gardening, animals and plants, observing and identifying environmental features
Visual–Spatial A child who thinks in images, colours and shapes. He/she learns best through activities involving visualisation.		art, craft and design, watching films, interpreting images, visual puzzles or games
Bodily–Kinaesthetic A child with good physical awareness. He/she learns best through 'hands-on' activities.		craft, motor coordination, sports skills, acting, demonstrations, taking objects apart and putting them back together
Musical–Rhythmic A child with an awareness of rhythm and sound. He/she learns best through activities involving music or rhythms.		playing musical instruments, singing, rhythm, identification of sounds, interpreting music, chants
Interpersonal A child who enjoys being in groups and teams. He/she learns best through activities involving working with others.		friendship qualities, being a leader, playing team sports, group work and showing empathy for others
Intrapersonal A child who understands and analyses his/her thoughts and feelings. He/she learns best through individual activities.		identifying beliefs, expressing feelings, working alone, personal challenges, setting and reaching goals

Teachers notes

Implications of multiple intelligences for teaching

In the traditional western education system, a child's intelligence is largely measured by his/her linguistic and mathematical abilities. This undervalues abilities and achievements in other curriculum areas. The theory of multiple intelligences, in contrast, values equally a range of different intelligences and thereby acknowledges individual differences. If teachers accept Gardner's theory, it has implications for the way they plan, present and assess child work.

Setting up a multiple intelligences classroom

- Research schools that use a multiple intelligences approach by visiting their websites. Try:

  http://www.gardnerschool.org
  http://www.newcityschool.org/home.html
  http://cookps.act.edu.au/mi.htm

  More schools can be found by typing 'multiple intelligence school' into a search engine. (Please note that the above websites were in operation at the time of publication.)

- Create intelligence profiles for your class by identifying each child's dominant intelligence(s). This can be done formally or informally.
  Some formal tests can be found on the Internet. Try:

  http://www.mitest.com/omitest.htm
  http://cortland.edu/psych/mi/measure.html
  (will need adapting to a child's level)

  More tests can be found by typing 'multiple intelligence checklist' into a search engine. (Please note that the above websites were in operation at the time of publication.)

  Informal methods may include observing work habits, asking children about their interests and hobbies, holding parent–teacher conferences, talking to other teachers or reading a child's previous school records. A series of checklists to help identify a child's dominant intelligence(s) is also provided on pages x – xi.

- Identify your own dominant intelligence(s) (and, therefore, your teaching approach) by using the checklist on page ix. Use the results to help you decide on the most effective teaching/learning tools for you. You may also like to consider team teaching with other staff members who are dominant in different intelligences. Remember that although you don't have to teach/learn every concept in eight different ways, it is important to develop other teaching styles or intelligences to cater for children who may have different strengths from yours.

- Educate children about multiple intelligences and allow them to discover their own strengths and weaknesses. Discuss how everyone is 'wise' in a different way and encourage children to work on their weaknesses. During lessons, show that you value individual differences.

- Allow children to tutor other children using their strong intelligences.

- Encourage children to use their dominant intelligences to aid understanding of topics that would usually require using a weaker intelligence.

- Use a range of methods to assess child work; e.g. traditional tests, role-play, work samples, portfolios. The methods you choose should allow children to demonstrate their intelligence strengths. Some assessment proformas are found on pages xii – xiii.

Teachers notes

- Plan cross-curricular units of work that allow children to use all the intelligences. One suggested method of doing this is to brainstorm ideas for each intelligence on a particular topic. For example:

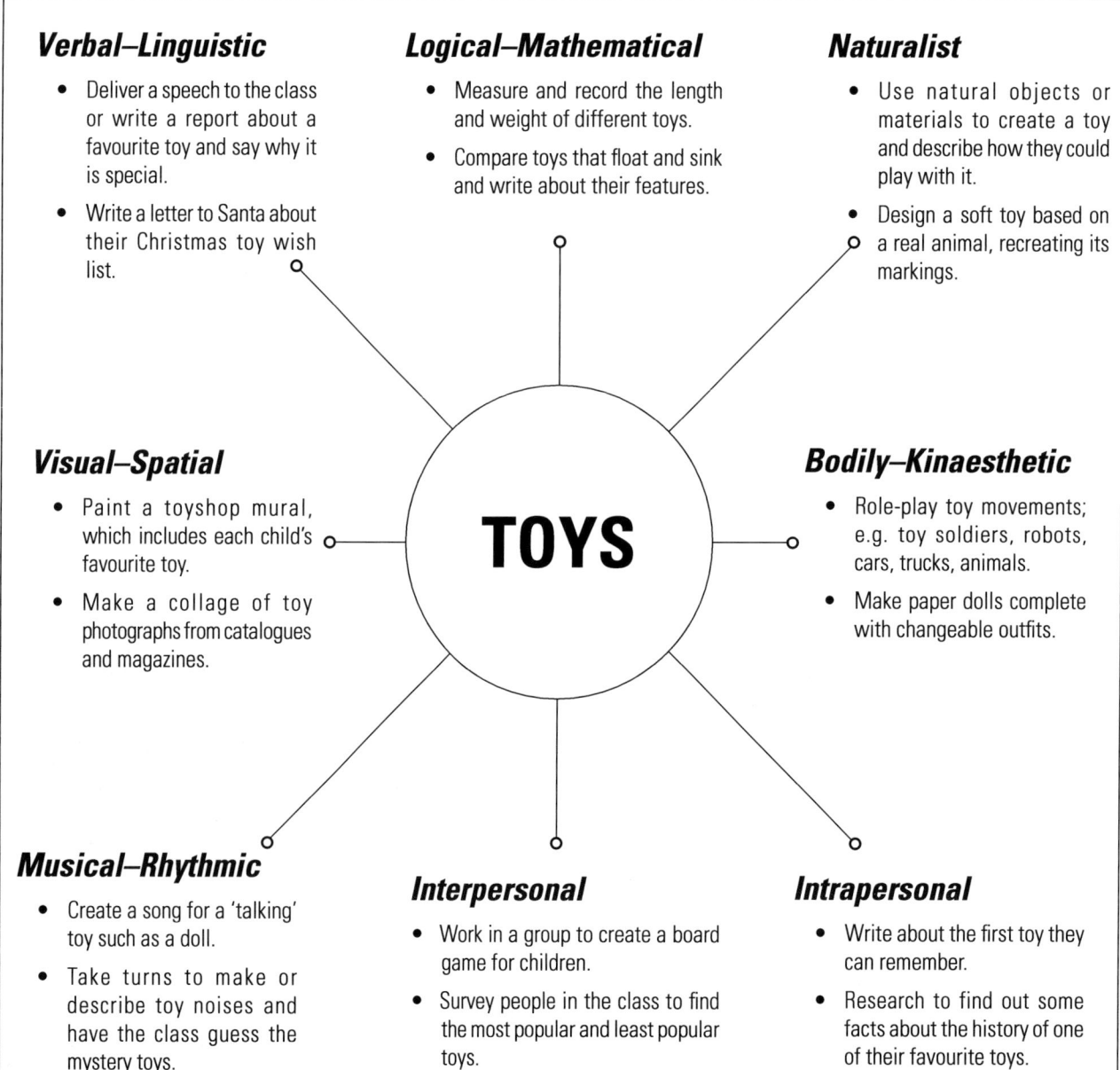

Verbal–Linguistic
- Deliver a speech to the class or write a report about a favourite toy and say why it is special.
- Write a letter to Santa about their Christmas toy wish list.

Logical–Mathematical
- Measure and record the length and weight of different toys.
- Compare toys that float and sink and write about their features.

Naturalist
- Use natural objects or materials to create a toy and describe how they could play with it.
- Design a soft toy based on a real animal, recreating its markings.

Visual–Spatial
- Paint a toyshop mural, which includes each child's favourite toy.
- Make a collage of toy photographs from catalogues and magazines.

Bodily–Kinaesthetic
- Role-play toy movements; e.g. toy soldiers, robots, cars, trucks, animals.
- Make paper dolls complete with changeable outfits.

Musical–Rhythmic
- Create a song for a 'talking' toy such as a doll.
- Take turns to make or describe toy noises and have the class guess the mystery toys.

Interpersonal
- Work in a group to create a board game for children.
- Survey people in the class to find the most popular and least popular toys.

Intrapersonal
- Write about the first toy they can remember.
- Research to find out some facts about the history of one of their favourite toys.

TOYS

Remember that an activity or task is likely to involve more than one intelligence, but you can choose to focus on a particular intelligence.

Another form of planning an overview is illustrated below.

				Toys			
Verbal–Linguistic	**Logical–Mathematical**	**Naturalist**	**Visual–Spatial**	**Bodily–Kinaesthetic**	**Musical–Rhythmic**	**Interpersonal**	**Intrapersonal**
Deliver a speech to the class or write a report about a favourite toy and say why it is special. Write a letter to Santa about their Christmas toy wish list.	Measure and record the length and weight of different toys. Compare toys that float and sink and write about their features.	Use natural objects or materials to create a toy and describe how they could play with it. Design a soft toy based on a real animal, recreating its markings.	Paint a toyshop mural, which includes each child's favourite toy. Make a collage of toy photographs from catalogues and magazines.	Role-play toy movements; e.g. toy soldiers, robots, cars, trucks, animals. Make paper dolls complete with changeable outfits.	Create a song for a 'talking' toy such as a doll. Take turns to make or describe toy noises and have the class guess the mystery toys.	Work in a group to create a board game for children. Survey people in the class to find the most popular and least popular toys.	Write about the first toy they can remember. Research to find out some facts about the history of one of their favourite toys.

How to use this book

This book contains six units of work, each of which covers a single topic.
The topics are:

Mini-beasts	Transport	The sea	Toys	Community	Me

Each unit consists of the following pages:

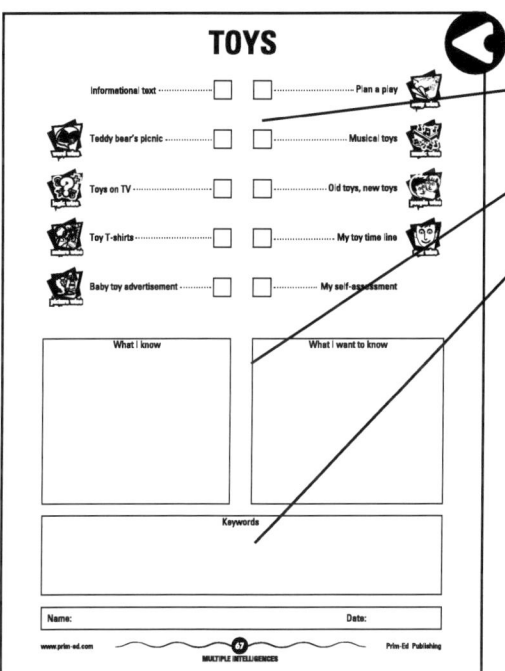

The first page of each unit is a **cover page** designed for the children. It can be glued into children's workbooks at the beginning of the unit. Children can fill in the tick boxes to indicate which worksheets and subsequent intelligences have been completed.

Before the children begin work on the unit, they should complete these sections individually. Teachers may ask children to brainstorm possible answers as a class or in small groups first.

A keyword section is provided for children to list words or phrases important to the subject. Children may begin by writing a few and adding to the list as they work through the unit. The words or phrases can be typed directly into the children's preferred Internet search engine to promote the most appropriate response to the topic.

An **overview** for teachers has been included for each unit to provide ideas for activities that focus on each intelligence. Teachers could use these activities to further develop the unit topic with the class or as extension work for more able children.

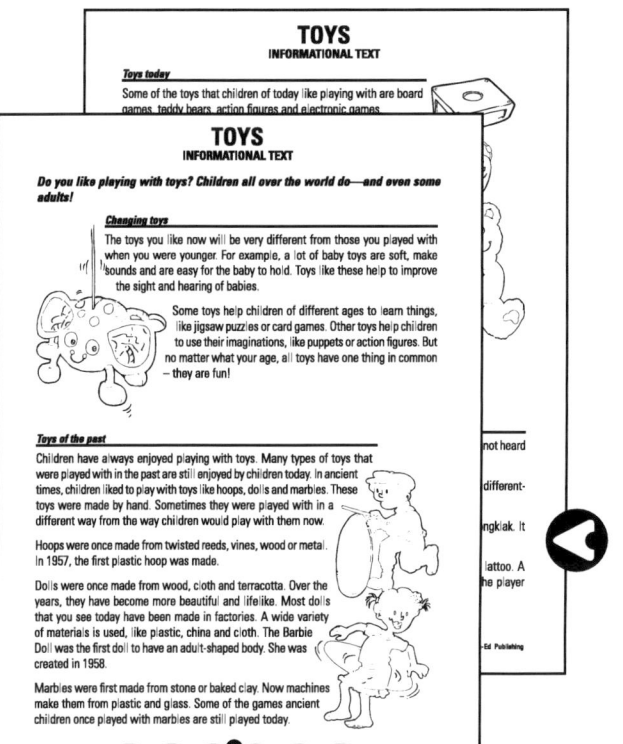

Two pages of general **informational text** about the topic have been provided, written at a child's level of understanding. This text could be used in variety of ways. For example:

- to provide information the children can use in the worksheets,
- for comprehension exercises,
- as a springboard for research projects,
- as a stimulus for class or group discussions.

How to use this book

Eight worksheets are contained in each unit. Each worksheet has been designed to focus on a single intelligence. However, as Gardner has pointed out, every activity we do requires the use of more than one intelligence. Therefore, teachers will be able to identify other intelligences operating as the children complete the worksheets.

It is advisable that teachers use each worksheet in the unit to ensure that all the intelligences have been covered.

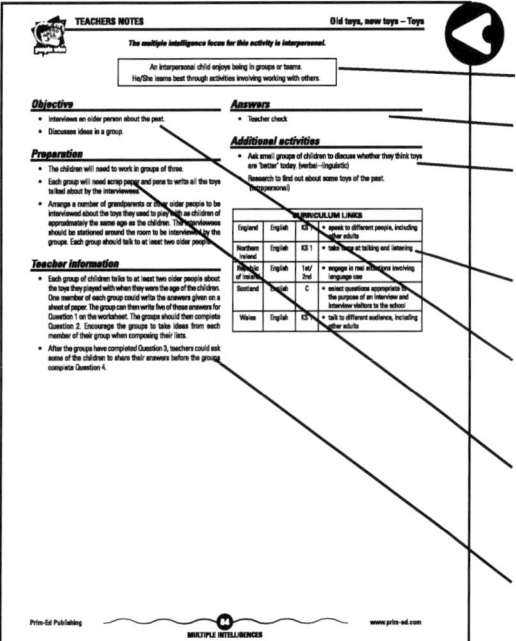

Each worksheet has an accompanying teachers page.

General information about the dominant intelligence is provided.

Answers, if required, are included.

Additional activities are suggested to further develop the skills and/or concepts taught during the activity. Some of the additional activities will focus on a different intelligence to that of the worksheet—if so, this is indicated.

Curriculum links appropriate to each country are provided across the main learning area that best represents the intelligence being explored.

One or more **objectives** are given for each activity page, providing the teacher with the focus for the activity and the behaviours the children should be demonstrating by completing the activity.

Preparation details what needs to be done before the teacher introduces the activity page to the children. Some materials and preparations are required, others are suggestions.

Teacher information provides any information needed to use the worksheet most effectively. It may include background information or suggestions on how to organise the lesson.

The **task** and **multiple intelligence** for each worksheet are provided at the top of the page for the child's information.

The **activities** have been selected to focus on the multiple intelligence indicated and cover a range of curriculum areas.

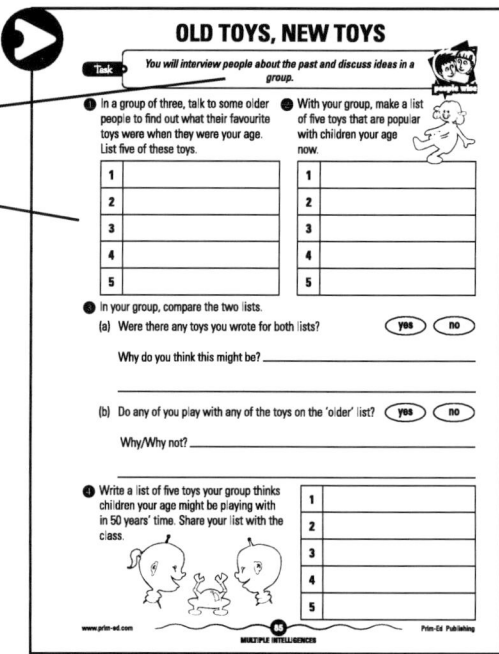

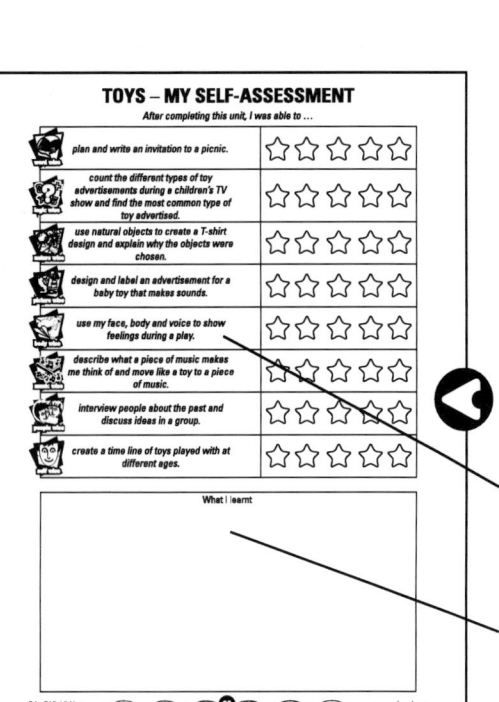

A **child assessment** page completes each unit. It should be given to the children when all the worksheets have been finished.

The children assess their work on the unit by colouring in the stars (with five stars being the best).

What I learnt can be completed after the children have brainstormed ideas in small groups or after a class discussion.

Teacher self-assessment proforma

Find out the intelligences in which you are strongest by ticking any statements that are true for you.

Verbal-Linguistic

I like to read during my leisure time. .... ❏

I enjoy teaching creative writing. .... ❏

I have strong verbal communication skills. .... ❏

I am skilled at teaching reading skills. .... ❏

Logical-Mathematical

I enjoy questioning how things work. .... ❏

I am an organised, logical person. .... ❏

I enjoy teaching number skills. .... ❏

I enjoy problem-solving activities. .... ❏

Naturalist

I enjoy caring for animals. .... ❏

I enjoy gardening. .... ❏

I am interested in environmental issues. .... ❏

I like teaching science lessons involving nature or natural forces. .... ❏

Visual-Spatial

I enjoy teaching art and craft. .... ❏

I am skilled in making or building things. .... ❏

I can easily picture creative ideas in my head. .... ❏

I am skilled at drawing or painting. .... ❏

Bodily-Kinaesthetic

I enjoy teaching physical education. .... ❏

I am skilled at dancing or acting. .... ❏

I enjoy activities that require fine gross motor skills. .... ❏

I regularly play a sport for enjoyment. .... ❏

Musical-Rhythmic

I play a musical instrument or sing well. .... ❏

I regularly use music and rhythms in the classroom. .... ❏

I can successfully teach children musical concepts. .... ❏

I enjoy listening to music. .... ❏

Interpersonal

I have a wide circle of friends. .... ❏

I am skilled at teaching children how to develop good relationships with others. .... ❏

I am a natural leader. .... ❏

I enjoy working in a group or team. .... ❏

Intrapersonal

I regularly set and achieve personal goals. .... ❏

I like teaching lessons about feelings and emotions. .... ❏

I usually enjoy the time I spend alone. .... ❏

I have strong beliefs and opinions. .... ❏

Which intelligences did you score the most ticks in? _____

Use these results to reflect on how you teach and how you might change your teaching style to incorporate all of the intelligences.

ix

MULTIPLE INTELLIGENCES

Prim-Ed Publishing

Assessment of child learning styles proforma – 1

Highlight any statements that describe the child's behaviours or skills.
Write any other appropriate behaviours or skills you have observed.

Child name:

Verbal–Linguistic

The child:

- achieves outstanding results in English.
- enjoys writing stories or poems.
- has an excellent vocabulary.
- enjoys reading.
- is skilled at word games.
- enjoys being read to.
- is skilled at verbal communication.

Other:

Naturalist

The child:

- likes to talk about his/her pets.
- enjoys natural science lessons.
- is fascinated with plants.
- brings natural objects to class to talk about.
- enjoys learning about animals.
- enjoys learning about the environment.

Other:

Logical–Mathematical

The child:

- has excellent number skills.
- enjoys logic puzzles and games.
- often questions how things work.
- is a competent problem-solver.
- enjoys science experiments.
- likes playing board games.
- can organise objects into logical groups.

Other:

Visual–Spatial

The child:

- enjoys art and craft lessons.
- interprets visual texts more easily than words.
- is a daydreamer.
- is skilled at making models.
- often doodles on work.
- enjoys viewing films or pictures.
- enjoys completing visual puzzles like mazes.

Other:

Assessment of child learning styles proforma – 2

Highlight any statements that describe the child's behaviours or skills.
Write any other appropriate behaviours or skills you have observed.

Child name:

Bodily–Kinaesthetic

The child:

- enjoys physical education lessons.
- has excellent coordination skills.
- has a talent for acting.
- is skilled at craft activities.
- enjoys hands-on activities.
- moves or fidgets at his/her desk.
- enjoys taking objects apart and putting them back together.

Other:

Interpersonal

The child:

- is a natural leader.
- prefers to work in groups or teams.
- has a wide circle of friends.
- is empathetic to others.
- belongs to clubs or other groups.
- enjoys helping others.

Other:

Musical–Rhythmic

The child:

- can play a musical instrument.
- enjoys singing or chanting.
- likes listening to music.
- taps feet or fingers when working.
- demonstrates a good sense of rhythm.
- hums to himself/herself.
- creates his/her own songs.

Other:

Intrapersonal

The child:

- enjoys working on his/her own.
- likes to think about his/her feelings.
- shows independent thought or action.
- can easily express his/her feelings or opinions.
- has a good sense of his/her abilities.
- can set and reach personal goals.

Other:

Child self-assessment of learning styles proforma – 1

What kind of learner are you? Tick the sentences that are true for you.

Am I word wise?

I love to read books............................ ❑

I like writing stories and poems. .... ❑

Word puzzles and games are fun........ ❑

I am good at spelling. .... ❑

I enjoy telling news........................... ❑

I like learning new words. .... ❑

Am I body wise?

I like playing sport............................. ❑

I find it hard to sit still at my desk. ..... ❑

Drama is lots of fun. .... ❑

I like to know what objects feel like... ❑

I like making things with my hands. ... ❑

I prefer to 'do' rather than watch. ...... ❑

Am I logic wise?

I like to know how things work........... ❑

I love board games like chess............. ❑

I enjoy science experiments. .... ❑

I like puzzles that make me think........ ❑

I like trying to solve problems............. ❑

Number games are fun. .... ❑

Am I picture wise?

Art is my favourite subject.................. ❑

I like to do jigsaw puzzles. .... ❑

I am good at drawing. .... ❑

I can read maps easily. .... ❑

I enjoy making models. .... ❑

I often have vivid dreams.................... ❑

Am I nature wise?

I have a collection of shells, rocks or other natural objects..❑

I like to care for animals. .... ❑

I enjoy gardening. .... ❑

I love to visit museums or zoos... ❑

I prefer to be outdoors rather than indoors. .... ❑

Looking after the environment is important to me............... ❑

Child self-assessment of learning styles proforma – 2

What kind of learner are you? Tick the sentences that are true for you.

Am I music wise?

I like to sing. .... ❏

I play, or would like to play, a musical instrument. .... ❏

When I work, I often tap my feet or my fingers. .... ❏

I enjoy listening to music. .... ❏

I know lots of songs off by heart. .... ❏

I enjoy listening to rhymes/raps. .... ❏

Am I people wise?

I enjoy team sports. .... ❏

I like to work in a group. .... ❏

I like sharing my ideas with others. .... ❏

I have more than three close friends. .... ❏

I find it interesting to meet new people. .... ❏

When people around me are happy it makes me feel happy too. .... ❏

Am I self wise?

I do my best schoolwork on my own. .... ❏

I often think about what I will do when I grow up. .... ❏

Staying home is usually more fun than being in a crowd of people. .... ❏

I have one or two close friends. .... ❏

I like to think about how I feel. .... ❏

I write in a diary in my free time. .... ❏

❷ Most of your ticks should be in one or two learning styles. Which learning style(s) has/have the most ticks? Circle the icon(s).

❸ Complete these sentences.

(a) I have found I am a _____ learner.

(b) Look at the learning styles which you ticked the least. Which of these learning styles would you most like to work on?

MINI-BEASTS

Informational text ········ ☐   ☐ ········ Make a mini-beast

body wise

word wise

Mini-beast report ········ ☐   ☐ ········ Mini-beast sound effects

music wise

logic wise

Classifying mini-beasts ········ ☐   ☐ ········ Mini-beast survey

people wise

nature wise

Mini-beast hunt ········ ☐   ☐ ········ Invent a mini-beast

self wise

picture wise

Mini-beast life cycle ········ ☐   ☐ ········ My self-assessment

What I know	What I want to know

Keywords

Name: Date:

MINI-BEASTS OVERVIEW

Verbal–Linguistic

- Have each child bring a mini-beast to class and talk about its features.
- Write a 'day in the life' of a small garden creature, thinking about the dangers it might encounter.
- Write a talk given by a spider or caterpillar complaining about the use of insect spray or the inconvenience of living with humans.
- Relate an instance of being confronted by a scary spider or insect.
- Read books about mini-beasts.
- Write reports about a mini-beast.
- Explain how to treat a bee sting.
- Write an acrostic poem using the name of a mini-beast.
- Make a list of verbs telling what different mini-beasts do.
- Write a newspaper article about a 'Giant _____ (insect of choice)' found in a remote area.
- Write 'Who am I's?' about mini-beasts.
- Write a profile for a 'new' mini-beast.

Naturalist

- Set up and study an ant farm.
- Find out which mini-beasts are endangered and which are considered to be pests.
- Go into the playground to observe mini-beasts.
- Research useful, harmful, noisy etc. mini-beasts.
- Collect 'bugs' in bug catchers to study (and then let go).
- Draw a diagram of a mini-beast, including labels and special features.
- Find out about mini-beasts that are useful to humans. Make a list and tell why each creature is useful.
- Insecticides are used to kill many different mini-beasts. Explain why this is necessary or why you think it isn't.
- Explain how earthworms help gardeners.
- Make a list of the enemies of different mini-beasts.
- Keep various mini-beasts in the class for children to observe.
- Construct homes to keep mini-beasts; e.g. woodlice, caterpillars, silkworms.
- Research how mini-beasts see, feel, hear and move.

Logical–Mathematical

- Count the number of legs different mini-beasts have. Group those with two legs, six legs, more than 10 legs etc.
- Compare and contrast data about different mini-beasts.
- Collect data about a specific mini-beast and record under specific headings.
- Classify mini-beasts as flying, walking, hopping, swimming, crawling, sliding.
- Research information about the numbers of ants in a colony or bees in a hive.
- Research information about the life span of different mini-beasts.
- Research and compile mini-beast 'world records', e.g. the longest mini-beast, the strongest mini-beast.
- Draw a time line showing the life of a mini-beast.
- Classify mini-beasts by body parts, features, colours, protection or how they move.
- Observe mini-beasts in the local environment. Draw and record what you can see. Group and classify with other class results.

Visual–Spatial

- View the markings on a range of mini-beasts and use them to create symmetrical patterns.
- Explore how mini-beasts use camouflage to hide.
- Draw a scene in the garden showing different kinds of mini-beasts.
- Graph mini-beasts found in a picture.
- View a sequence of pictures about a mini-beast and place in the correct order to tell a simple story.
- Create a collage using pictures of mini-beasts cut from magazines.
- Draw a scary, imaginary mini-beast. Give your creature a name.
- Draw and label mini-beasts.
- Record and graph the types and numbers of mini-beasts found in a particular area of the school.
- Make a mobile of a mini-beast, showing its life cycle.
- Use 3-D recycled materials to build a mini-beast.
- Create blotting paper mini-beasts with ink blots, adding interesting features.
- Construct a 3-D life cycle of a mini-beast, using arrows to show the order of each stage.

MINI-BEASTS OVERVIEW

Musical–Rhythmic

- Listen to *The Flight of the Bumblebee* and create group movement pieces to it.
- Sing songs or recite poems about small creatures; e.g. 'Ladybird, Ladybird', 'Incy Wincy Spider', 'Alexander Beetle' etc.
- Create patterns or lines on paper to music. Use these to make art and craft works of mini-beasts.
- Make a list of mini-beasts that make noises. Do any of them sing? How do they make sounds?
- Make and perform a butterfly dance. Choose appropriate sounds or music.
- Produce a concert about mini-beasts in the garden.

Interpersonal

- In a group, collect materials to recreate the natural habitats of a range of mini-beasts in shoeboxes.
- After a class discussion, have small groups of children role-play what they would do if they were stung or bitten by some mini-beasts.
- In pairs, role-play, 'Little Miss Muffet' and other rhymes or songs with mini-beasts in them.
- In a group, tell the story about 'A day in the life of _____ (choose a mini-beast)'.
- Work with a partner to list five differences between spiders and insects.
- In a small group, find out why mosquitoes are dangerous to humans.
- Survey class members to find the favourite and/or least favourite mini-beast.

Bodily–Kinaesthetic

- Mime being an insect caught in a bug catcher and then rescued.
- Make models of mini-beasts using everyday materials.
- Perform action rhymes such as 'Incy, Wincy, Spider', 'Fuzzy Wuzzy Caterpillar' etc.
- Move to indicate different mini-beasts; e.g. caterpillar, worm, snail, spider.
- Mime (in pairs) the drama of a spider spinning a web, trapping a fly and the consequences.
- Do morning fitness as if you were a _____ (choose a mini-beast).
- Make spider webs to display. Attach 3-D spiders.
- Grow a 'hairy' caterpillar using open-hole cloth tubes filled with birdseed.

Intrapersonal

- Have the children write about which mini-beast they would most like to be.
- Write about how you feel about spiders etc.
- Select a mini-beast to research and write a report.
- Create a life cycle in pictures and words for a specific mini-beast.
- Choose any mini-beast. What would this animal think about humans? Should humans treat it better? Explain why you think this.
- Invent your own mini-beast. Include a description, labelled diagram, what it does, what it eats, where it lives etc.
- Prepare a plan to care for a mini-beast.

MINI-BEASTS
INFORMATIONAL TEXT

Snails

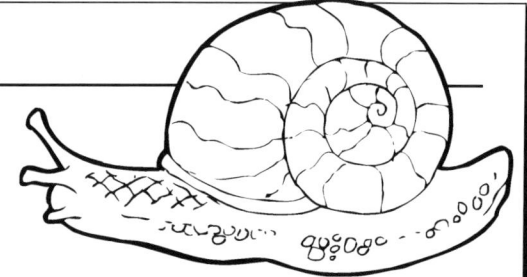

Snails are molluscs.

Snails are related to slugs. Snails have a large coiled shell, a large foot, a head with eyes and tentacles.

Snails can be found all over the world. Some snails live on land, while others live in the sea or freshwater ponds.

Snails like to eat plants. They leave a trail of mucus behind them when they move.

Some snails are:
freshwater snails
land snails
sea snails

Worms

Worms are invertebrates.

A worm has a head at one end, a tail at the other and many body segments. Each body segment is the same.

Most worms burrow in the soil and are found all over the world. They hardly ever leave their burrows so they won't get eaten by birds or other animals.

Worms move by making each segment long and thin or short and fat in turn.

Some types of worms are:
earthworms
leeches
roundworms

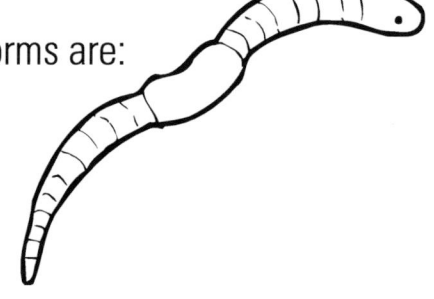

Millipedes and centipedes

Millipedes and centipedes are arthropods.

They have many body segments, each with one or two pairs of legs. Centipedes have about 16 pairs of legs. Millipedes never have a thousand legs; the most legs a millipede has been found to have is 750.

Millipedes and centipedes prefer humid, damp climates.
Centipedes are carnivores, with large jaws to eat their prey. Millipedes are herbivores, eating soil, plants, algae and moss.

MINI-BEASTS
INFORMATIONAL TEXT

Insects

Flies, beetles, mosquitoes, moths, butterflies, crickets, bees, dragonflies, grasshoppers, stick insects, cockroaches, bugs, wasps and ants are all insects.

All insects have six legs, a head, a thorax, an abdomen, antennae and eyes. Some insects also have wings.

Insects can be found all over the world and are the most common animal on the planet. Many plants with fruit or flowers are pollinated by insects which fly from one plant to another.

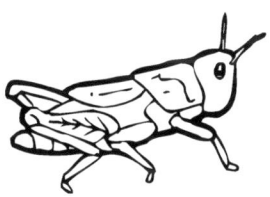

Insects begin life as an egg and change many times as they grow into an adult.

Spiders

Spiders are arachnids.

Spiders have a head, a thorax and four pairs of legs. Some spiders are poisonous.

Most spiders live in and around water.

Spiders use silk glands in their abdomen to spin webs, which help them to trap their food.

Some types of spiders are:

daddy-long-legs
huntsman
wolf
tarantulas
jumping
funnel-web
red-back

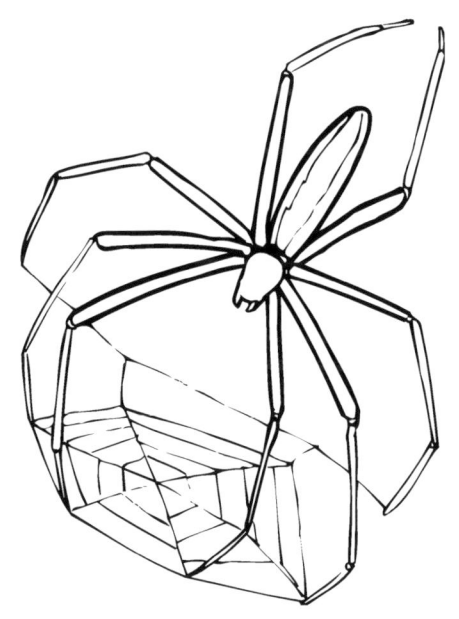

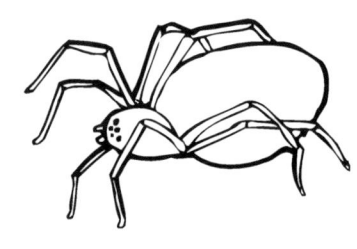

The multiple intelligence focus for this task is verbal–linguistic.

> A verbal–linguistic child thinks in words.
> He/She learns best through activities involving reading, writing and speaking.

Objective

- Writes a report about a mini-beast.

Preparation

- Collect resource books on mini-beasts to provide children with the information they need.
- Some research could be done using the Internet.
- Some mini-beast information is provided on the information pages.

Teacher information

- Brainstorm, as a whole class, to find all the different mini-beasts children can think of. Record these on the board as a reference for all children.
- Revise the use of keywords and phrases in note-taking exercises.
- Demonstrate, with a short piece of text, how to extract keywords and phrases, recording them in the table for the report.
- Children can then select a mini-beast from the class list or use one of their own to research for the report.
- Allow children to peruse the resources to find information on their chosen mini-beast.
- Give children a set time to use the resources to complete the keywords and phrases in their report framework.
- Children then use the information recorded to write a draft of their report.
- At this point, it is important to revise drafting and editing procedures with the children. Remind children of the importance of correct spelling and punctuation. Encourage children to read their own work to check if it makes sense, and to swap with a partner and check each other's work.
- Children can then present their final draft. Remind them that it is also a good idea to include diagrams with labels in a report.

Answers

Teacher check

Additional activities

- Children can present their report orally to the class. (verbal–linguistic)
- Children can make a piece of music to suit the mini-beast they chose to report on. (musical–rhythmic)

CURRICULUM LINKS			
England	Literacy	Yr 1/2	• write non-chronological reports
Northern Ireland	English	KS 1	• write for a range of purposes, including a report
Republic of Ireland	English	1st/ 2nd	• write in a variety of genres
Scotland	English	B	• write reports, using simple notes to order writing
Wales	English	KS 1	• write in a range of forms

MINI-BEAST REPORT

You will write a report about a mini-beast.

1 Choose a mini-beast you would like to find out more about.

2 Use keywords and phrases to plan your mini-beast report below.

word wise

Title What is it called?	
Classification What is it called?	
Description What does it have? What does it look like?	
Location Where can it be found?	
Dynamics What does it do? What does it eat? How does it move?	

3 Present your mini-beast report on a separate sheet of paper.

The multiple intelligence focus for this task is logical–mathematical.

> A logical–mathematical child thinks rationally and in abstractions.
> He/She learns best through activities involving problem-solving, numbers and patterns.

Objective

- Classifies pictures of mini-beasts according to own grouping.

Preparation

- Children will need scissors and a reminder about how to use them safely.
- Children should put their initials on the back of each square prior to cutting out. In this way, if pieces are lost, the owner can easily be identified.
- Children will also need glue and a separate sheet of paper to glue their mini-beasts onto after classifying.

Teacher information

- Prior to cutting out the mini-beasts, direct children to look at each creature. As a class, discuss different ways the mini-beasts could be grouped.
- Direct children to cut out the mini-beasts and sort them according to how they would like them classified.
- Once children are happy with their own classification, glue the mini-beasts accordingly on a separate sheet of paper.
- Children can then write a reason why they classified the mini-beasts in the way that they have.

Answers

- Teacher check

Additional activities

- Move into a small group and discuss the way each child has classified his/her mini-beast. Are there any other ways the mini-beasts could be classified? (interpersonal)
- Create a mural of a garden and include the mini-beasts children have used in their classification. (visual–spatial)

CURRICULUM LINKS			
England	Science	KS 1	• group living things according to observable similarities and differences
Northern Ireland	Science	KS 1	• sort living things into groups using observable features
Republic of Ireland	Science	1st/ 2nd	• sort and group living things into sets according to observable features
Scotland	Science	A	• sort living things into broad groups according to easily observable characteristics
Wales	Science	KS 1	• group animals according to observable similarities and differences

CLASSIFYING MINI-BEASTS

Task • You will classify the pictures of mini-beasts according to your own classification.

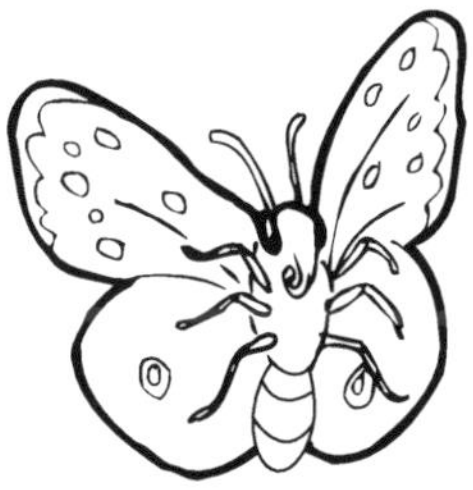

butterfly	ant	spider	worm
grasshopper	moth	centipede	snail
woodlouse	caterpillar	dragonfly	scorpion
fly	silkworm	bee	ladybird
cockroach	beetle	mosquito	stick insect

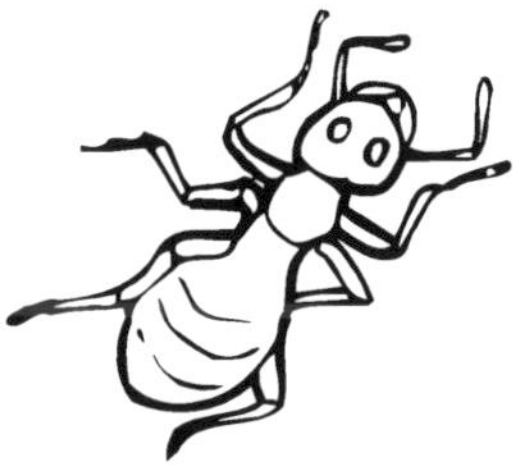

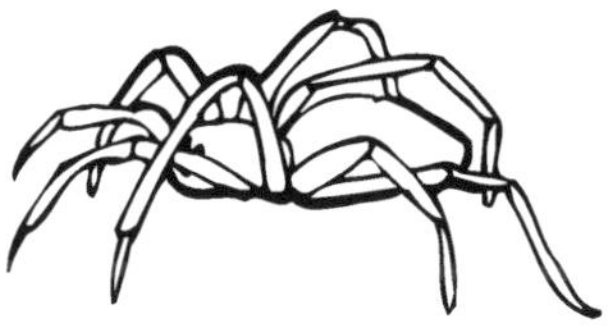

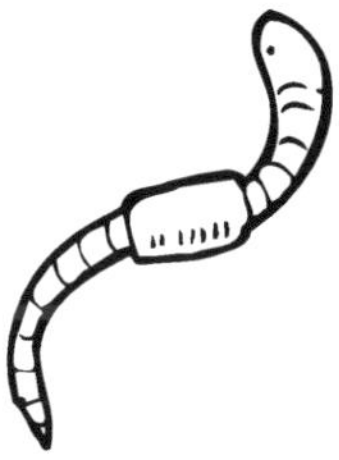

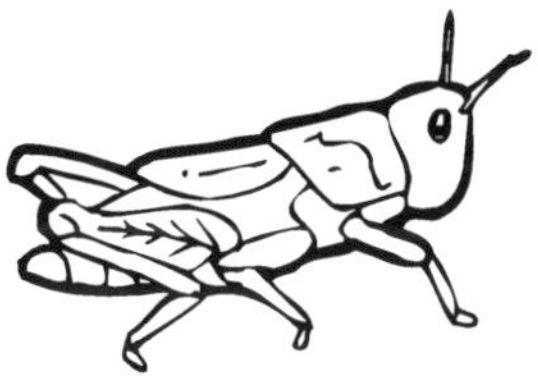

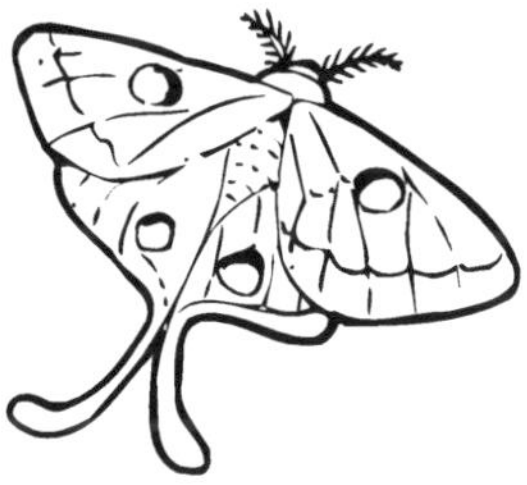

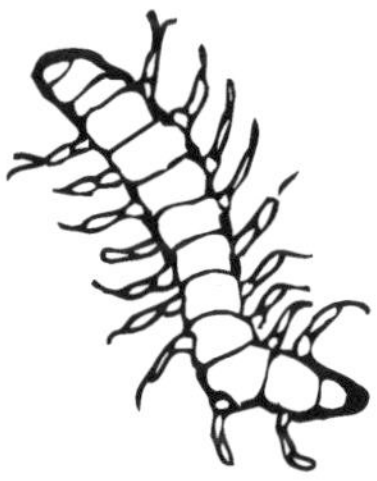

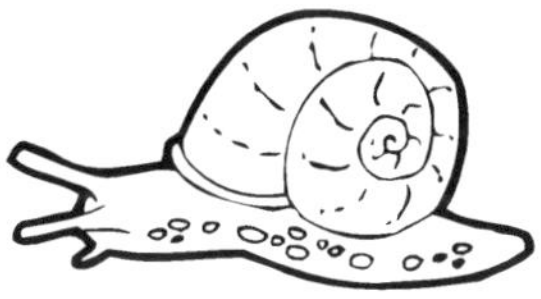

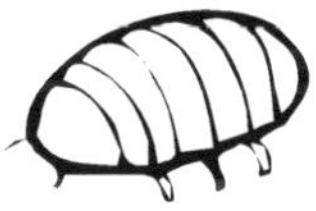

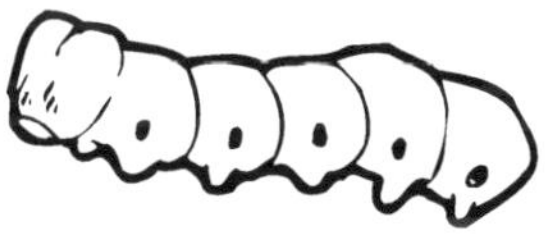

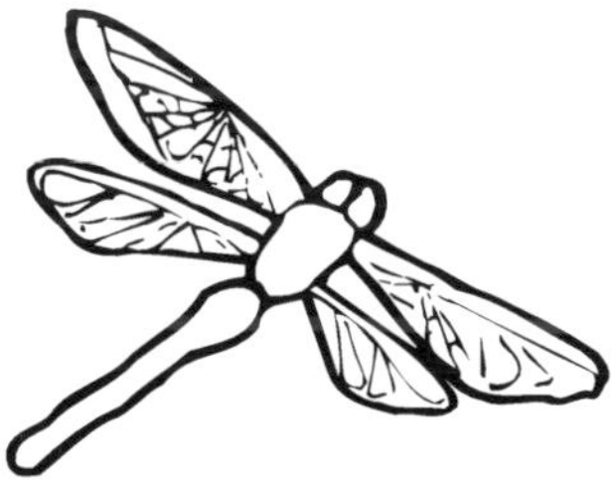

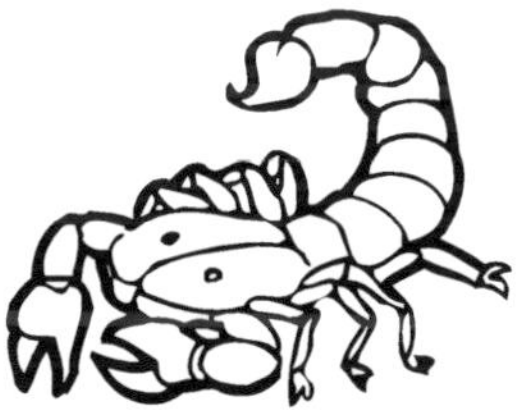

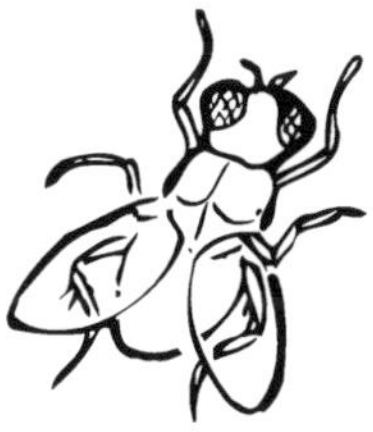

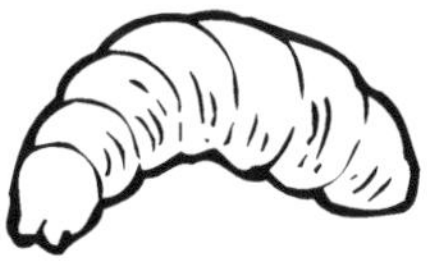

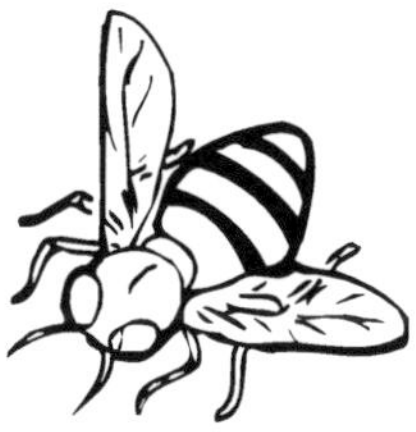

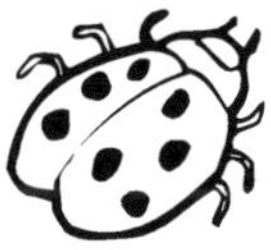

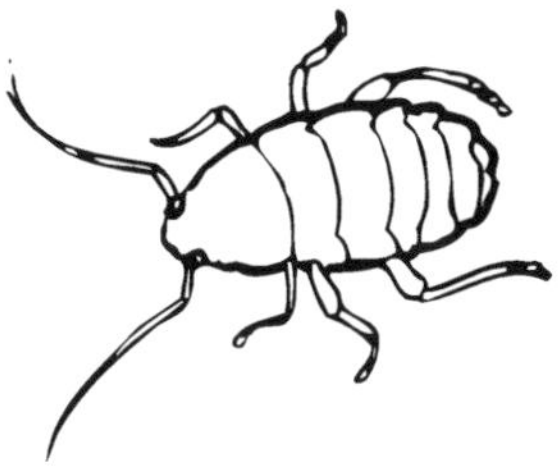

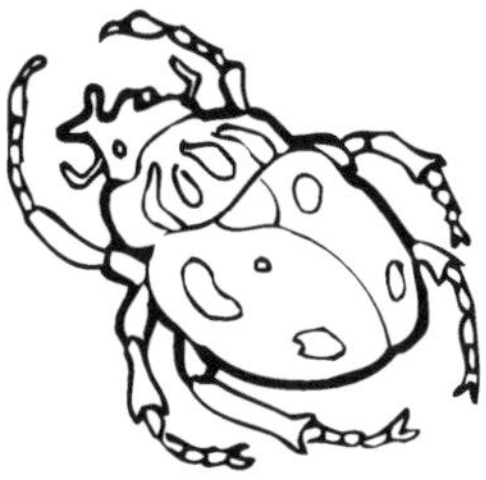

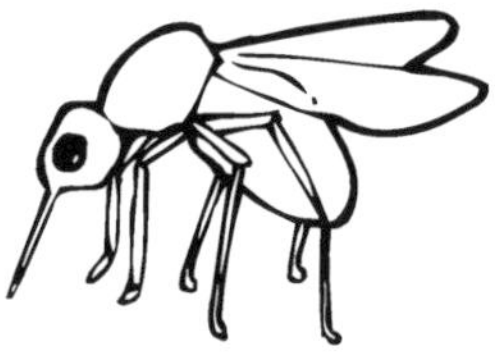

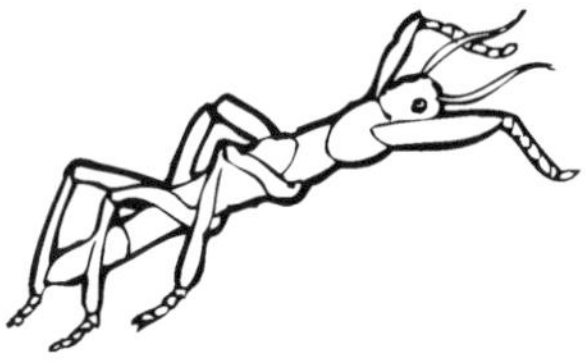

The multiple intelligence focus for this task is naturalist.

A naturalist child has an awareness of the patterns in nature.
He/She learns best through activities involving animals, plants and the environment.

Objective

- Observes mini-beasts in their natural environment and records observations.

Preparation

- Children will need to be organised into groups of four in order to share resources, but should record their results independently.

- A hoop can be used to define an area to 'hunt' for mini-beasts. If nothing can be found, move the hoop to another area. Magnifying glasses can be used to study the smaller mini-beasts.

Teacher information

- Prior to going outside to 'hunt' for mini-beasts, a group discussion of rules for working outside should be held. These include:

    - Keep the noise down, so as not to disturb other classes.
    - Remain on school property at all times.
    - Stay with your own group.
    - Report any accidents or mishaps to the teacher immediately.

- Brainstorm as a group to find the types of mini-beast children think they will find on their 'hunt'. Record these on the board. Further discuss where children think they may find particular types of mini-beasts. Will they be found on the ground?

- Children work in small groups to locate mini-beasts in the school grounds.

- Children then complete their recording sheets individually. Children may choose to record information about different mini-beasts from others in the group.

Answers

Answers will vary

Additional activities

- Write a complete report about the mini-beasts found on the mini-beast 'hunt'. (verbal–linguistic)
- Make a 3-D model of one of the mini-beasts found on the mini-beast 'hunt'. (bodily–kinaesthetic)

CURRICULUM LINKS			
England	Science	KS 1	• find out about the different kinds of animals in the local environment
Northern Ireland	Science	KS 1	• find out about the variety of animal life through direct observation
Republic of Ireland	Science	1st/2nd	• observe, identify and explore a variety of living things in local habitats and environments
Scotland	Science	A	• recognise and name some common animals found in the local environment
Wales	Science	KS 1	• find out about the different kinds of animals in the local environment

MINI-BEAST HUNT

Task *You will observe mini-beasts in their natural environment and record your observations below.*

1 Look around your school grounds to find different kinds of mini-beasts.

2 Draw and write about two mini-beasts in the boxes below.

A

What: _____

Where: _____

When: _____

What was it doing? _____

_____

_____

B

What: _____

Where: _____

When: _____

What was it doing? _____

_____

_____

3 Share your findings with another person in your class.

The multiple intelligence focus for this task is visual–spatial.

> A visual–spatial child thinks in images, colours and shape.
> He/She learns best through activities involving visualisation.

Objective

- Correctly orders the life cycle of a mini-beast.

Preparation

- Children will need a pair of scissors and glue to complete the activity.

Teacher information

- Display pictures showing the life cycle of a mini-beast. Discuss the various stages, what happens and how the mini-beast changes.

- Direct children to the worksheet. 'Which mini-beast life cycle is being shown here?'

- Read the text with the children.

- Children can colour the pictures before cutting out and gluing in order.

- Children then cut out the pictures and place them in the order they think over the life cycle wheel. Discuss their chosen order with a partner. Glue into place once children are happy with their order.

Answers

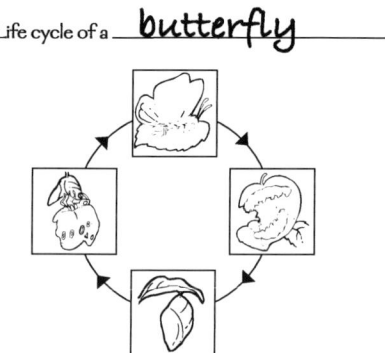

Life cycle of a *butterfly*

Additional activities

- Make a 3-D model showing the life cycle of a chosen mini-beast. (bodily–kinaesthetic)

- Work in pairs to present an interview between an interviewer and a mini-beast. Discuss how the mini-beast changes and how it feels at different stages of its life. (interpersonal)

CURRICULUM LINKS			
England	Science	KS 1	• know animals produce offspring, which grow into adults
Northern Ireland	Science	KS 1	• find out about animals and their young
Republic of Ireland	Science	1st/ 2nd	• become familiar with the life cycles of common animals
Scotland	Science	B	• recognise stages in the life cycles of familiar animals
Wales	Science	KS 1	• know animals produce offspring, which grow into adults

MINI-BEAST LIFE CYCLE

picture wise

1 Read the sentences.

2 Colour and cut out the pictures of the life cycle.

3 Glue the pictures in the correct places on the life cycle wheel.

Life cycle of a _____

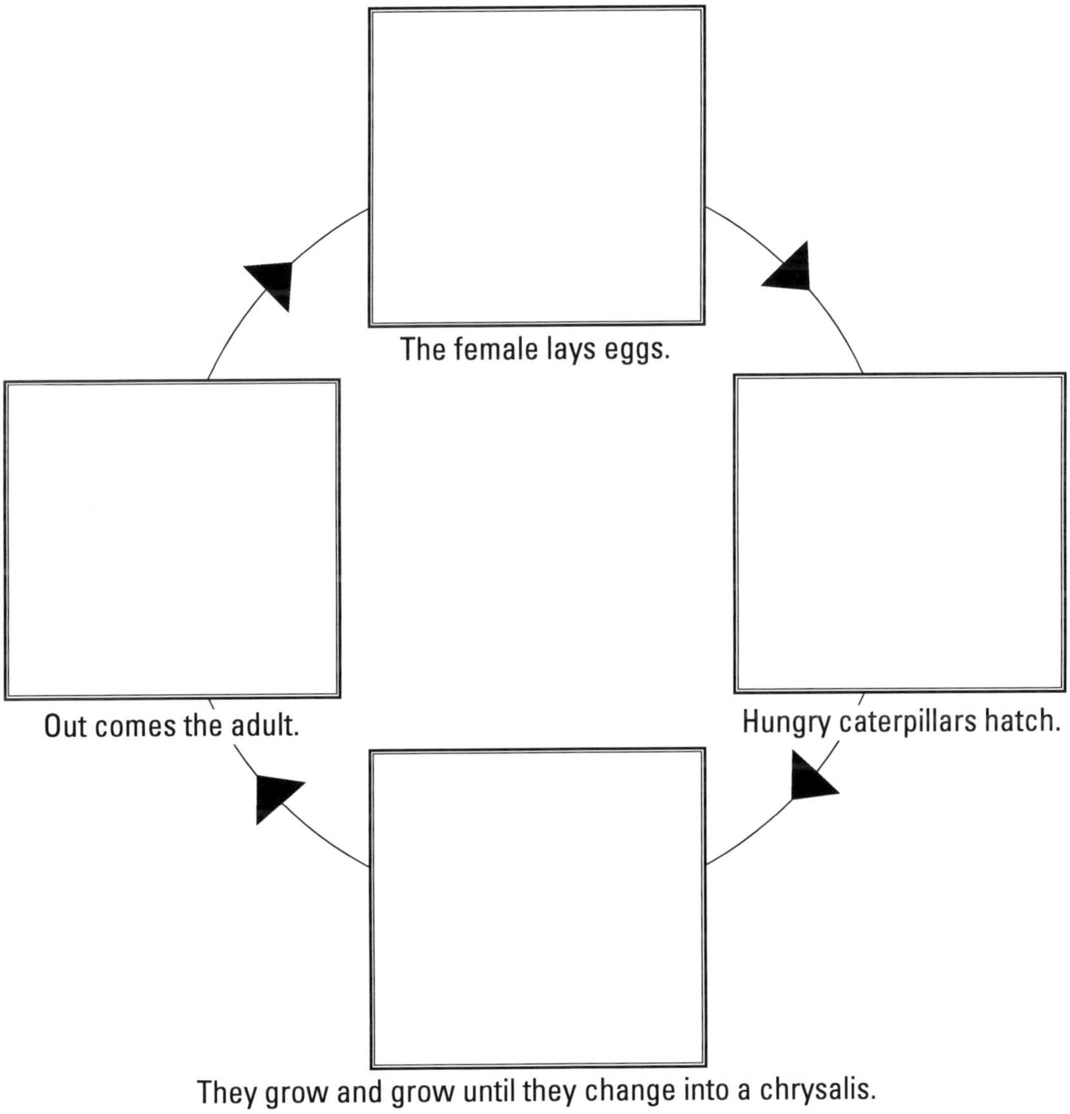

The female lays eggs.

Out comes the adult.

Hungry caterpillars hatch.

They grow and grow until they change into a chrysalis.

The multiple intelligence focus for this task is bodily–kinaesthetic.

> A bodily–kinaesthetic child has good physical awareness.
> He/She learns best through 'hands-on' activities.

Objective

- Uses recycled materials to make a 3-D model of his/her favourite mini-beast.

Teacher information

- Discuss different types of mini-beasts with children. Record a list of mini-beasts on the board.

- Look at the pictures and discuss the body parts: head, abdomen, thorax, antennae, eyes, legs, wings, tail and so on.

- Children decide which mini-beast they would like to make. Provide opportunities for child to locate a clear picture of their mini-beast.

- Children need to carefully plan how they are going to make their 3-D mini-beast (before making it). This involves completing the procedure on the worksheet.

- Children should be given the opportunity to rummage through recycled materials to get an idea of what they will use to make their mini-beast.

- Complete the procedure, then make the model of the mini-beast. In small groups, children can share techniques used to make the mini-beast and, if they need to, adjust their procedure in any way.

Answers

Teacher check

Additional activities

- Draw and paint the life cycle of your 3-D mini-beast. (visual–spatial)

- Add labels to your model naming the different parts of the mini-beast you made. (visual–linguistic)

CURRICULUM LINKS			
England	D & T	KS 1	• complete design and make assignments using a range of materials
Northern Ireland	Technology	KS 1	• plan what they are going to make and the materials they will use
Republic of Ireland	Science	1st/ 2nd	• communicate a plan of action and make simple objects
Scotland	Technology	B	• make a simple plan
Wales	D & T	KS 1	• complete tasks in which they design and make products

MAKE A MINI-BEAST

You will use recycled materials to make a 3-D model of your favourite mini-beast.

body wise

Name of mini-beast.		This is what it will look like.
What am I going to do?		
What materials will I use?		
How will I make my mini-beast?		
How did it turn out?	1 2 3 4 5 Not so well Fantastic!	
Notes:		

The multiple intelligence focus for this task is musical–rhythmic.

> A musical–rhythmic child has an awareness of music and sound.
> He/She learns best through activities involving music or rhythms.

Objective

- Creates mini-beast sound effects using musical instruments and natural resources.

Preparation

- Children can assist in collecting items suitable for sound effects, according to the particular mini-beast they choose.

Teacher information

- Children can choose to make the sound of a mini-beast and/or the sound of an action made by a mini-beast. This is recorded in Question 1.

- Discuss the use of adjectives or describing words. Select a mini-beast and brainstorm as a whole class to list the types of sounds it makes when it moves and when it 'talks'.

- As a whole class, consider the musical instruments and/or natural resources that could be used to make the different sounds the mini-beast makes.

- Children can then complete the activity on the worksheet.

- Children will need a quiet place to work out and practise their sound effects using instruments and natural resources.

- Allow children to form pairs to check and guess each other's sound effects.

- Provide children with the opportunity to record their sound effects. Play them back to the whole class.

Answers

Teacher check

Additional activities

- Listen to a nature recording and identify the sounds of various mini-beasts. (musical-rhythmic)

- Create a collage of the mini-beast chosen for the sound effects. (visual-spatial)

CURRICULUM LINKS			
England	Music	KS 1	• explore, choose and organise sounds and musical ideas
Northern Ireland	Music	KS 1	• create simple sound effects using single sounds
Republic of Ireland	Music	1st/ 2nd	• explore how the sounds of different instruments can suggest various sounds
Scotland	Music	A	• select appropriate sound sources and combine and link sounds to convey effect in a short invention
Wales	Music	KS 1	• create, select and organise sounds in response to different stimuli

MINI-BEAST SOUND EFFECTS

Task You will create mini-beast sound effects using musical instruments and natural resources.

1 I am going to make sound effects for _____.

2 Write words to describe the types of sounds your mini-beast makes.

3 What types of instruments could you use? Write your answers on the leaf.

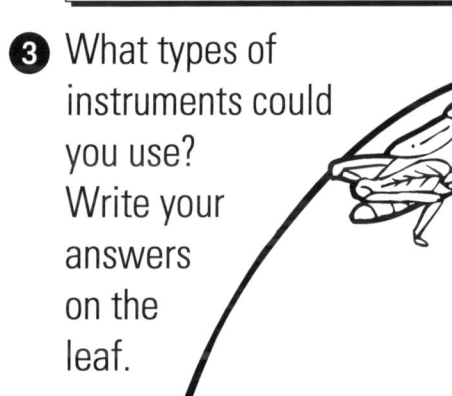

4 What natural resources could you use?

5 Practise your sound effects in a quiet place until you are happy with the sounds.

6 Ask a partner to listen to your sound effects. Can your partner tell what mini-beast you chose?

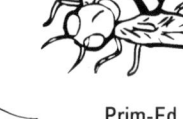

7 Record your sound effects and play them to the class.

The multiple intelligence focus for this task is interpersonal.

An interpersonal child enjoys being in groups or teams.
He/She learns best through activities involving working with others.

Objective

- Works in a small group to survey children in the school to find out the most popular and least popular mini-beast.

Preparation

- Check with other teachers in the school to see if they mind having an interruption to their day by allowing your children to survey their children.
- Organise the class into groups, so there are enough groups to survey each Year level in your school.

Teacher information

- Children will need to be familiar with appropriate survey techniques and manners in order to survey other classes within the school to collect results.
- Children record the members of their group and the class(es) they are responsible for surveying.
- Each group needs to work cooperatively to develop a survey question which will provide them with the information they need. Share each group's survey question and ensure it is clear before allowing them to go to other classes. Groups also need to include a list of mini-beasts they are going to survey. These mini-beasts should be the same for each group, to ensure results are comparable. This list may be developed as a whole class.
- Each group must nominate who will perform the following roles during the lesson: recorder, counter, speaker and reporter.
- Children survey other classes to gather data and return to class. An adult helper may be required with each group to ensure children perform the task accurately and appropriately.
- Each group then tallies its result to find the most and least popular mini-beasts for its survey class(es).
- Share each group's findings with the class.
- Discuss the findings and any variations or similarities among the classes.

Answers

Answers will vary

Additional activities

- Work in groups to compare and contrast the differences and similarities between moths and butterflies, bees and flies, snails and slugs, millipedes and centipedes, frogs and toads, and so on. (interpersonal)
- Work in groups to find out the most common type of mini-beast found in the school grounds. (interpersonal)

CURRICULUM LINKS			
England	Numeracy	Yr 1/2	• sort, classify and organise information in simple ways
Northern Ireland	Maths	KS 1	• collect, record, read and interpret data
Republic of Ireland	Maths	1st/ 2nd	• represent and interpret data
Scotland	Maths	C	• obtain information by conducting a survey which extends beyond the class, using a tally sheet
Wales	Maths	KS 1	• collect, record and interpret data

MINI-BEAST SURVEY

people wise

1 People in my group:

2 Survey class(es):

_____

3 Survey question: _____

_____

4 Results:

Name of mini-beast	Tally	Total

5 Most popular mini-beast   Least popular mini-beast

_____   _____

The multiple intelligence focus for this task is intrapersonal.

An intrapersonal child understands and analyses his/her thoughts and feelings. He/She learns best through individual activities.

Objective

• Uses knowledge of mini-beasts to invent his/her own.

Preparation

• Children may need to use the library or Internet resources to complete this activity.

Teacher information

• Children use the worksheet to record brief details about their mini-beast.

• Children will need to consider many aspects of their mini-beast and may need to refer to books and pictures.

Answers

Answers will vary

Additional activities

• Make a 3-D model of their invented mini-beast. (bodily-kinaesthetic)

• Prepare and present a talk about the mini-beast. (verbal-linguistic)

CURRICULUM LINKS			
England	Literacy	Yr2	• make simple notes
Northern Ireland	English	KS 1	• express imaginings
Republic of Ireland	English	1st/ 2nd	• write in a variety of genres
Scotland	English	B	• use simple notes
Wales	English	KS 1	• write in a range of forms

INVENT A MINI-BEAST

You will use your knowledge of mini-beasts to invent your own.

self wise

Name of mini-beast: _____

What does it look like?

_____

_____

_____

Draw your mini-beast here.

What colour(s) is it?

How big is it?

_____

Where does it live?

_____

How does it move?

What does it eat?

How does it grow and change?

How does it defend itself?

_____

MINI-BEASTS – MY SELF-ASSESSMENT

After using this unit, I was able to ...

word wise	write a report about a mini-beast.	☆ ☆ ☆ ☆ ☆
logic wise	classify pictures of mini-beasts according to my own grouping.	☆ ☆ ☆ ☆ ☆
nature wise	observe mini-beasts in their natural environment and record observations.	☆ ☆ ☆ ☆ ☆
picture wise	correctly order the life cycle of a mini-beast.	☆ ☆ ☆ ☆ ☆
body wise	use recycled materials to make a 3-D model of a favourite mini-beast.	☆ ☆ ☆ ☆ ☆
music wise	create mini-beast sound effects using musical instruments and natural resources.	☆ ☆ ☆ ☆ ☆
people wise	work in a small group to survey children in the school to find out the most popular and least popular mini-beast.	☆ ☆ ☆ ☆ ☆
self wise	use my knowledge of mini-beasts to invent my own.	☆ ☆ ☆ ☆ ☆

What I learnt

TRANSPORT

Informational text	☐ ☐	Make a helicopter **body wise**
word wise A travel adventure!	☐ ☐	Tuneful transport **music wise**
logic wise Air, land or water?	☐ ☐	Transport worker interview **people wise**
nature wise Transport problems	☐ ☐	Transport research **self wise**
picture wise Cruise ship uniform	☐ ☐	My self-assessment

What I know	What I want to know

Keywords

Name:	Date:

TRANSPORT OVERVIEW

Verbal–Linguistic

- Write messages using the International Phonetic Alphabet; e.g. 'a' = 'alpha', 'u' = 'uniform'.
- Invite a transport worker (e.g. pilot, hot air balloonist) to talk to the class about what he/she does.
- Read stories about cars, trains and buses; e.g. stories about Thomas the Tank Engine or Brum.
- Write a story about an old car being traded in for a newer model.
- Write instructions for travelling by train.
- Complete word searches that use different types of transport.
- Create 'What am I?' transport puzzles.
- Complete cloze passages of information about transport.
- Ask the children to imagine they have just been told the ferry they are on is sinking. They can then write the thoughts they might have and the actions they might take.
- Prepare a talk explaining which form of transport you would most like to use to get to school each day.

Naturalist

- Visit a transport museum, motor show or airport.
- Identify forms of transport in the past or present that do not cause pollution; e.g. walking, riding a horse, rafting, gliding.
- List five ways in which animal transport is better than transport that uses engines.
- Discuss ways to provide roads and train lines without destroying all the natural environment.

Logical–Mathematical

- Interpret transport timetables and use them to plan a trip.
- Note the types of transport that pass the school. Collate the information and create a graph.
- On a map of the world, label the places the children have visited. Place a car, bus, train, boat or plane picture next to each child's name to show the form of transport he/she used to get there.
- Make a time line of the evolution of transport. The time line should stretch around the classroom. It could concentrate on one form of transport or a variety of forms.
- Collect car advertisements from newspapers and order them according to different criteria; e.g. cost, power, age.
- List and explain some of the safety features of modern cars.
- Research air, land and water speed records.
- Research to find the biggest or the fastest aircraft or ship ever built. Record the size or maximum speed.

Visual–Spatial

- Draw and cut out pictures of different types of transport to create a collage.
- Design and make a poster encouraging children to walk to school more often or use public transport.
- Label an enlarged picture of a form of transport; e.g. a BMX bike or a mountain bike.
- Make charts of different types of transport used in different countries.
- Draw a map and then plan how to get to a favourite holiday destination.
- Create an advertisement to sell a bike. Include an illustration.
- Make a colourful sign that shows safety rules for bus or train passengers.
- Design a car of the future. Label its most interesting features.

TRANSPORT OVERVIEW

Bodily–Kinaesthetic

- Plan and perform group role-plays about people arriving late to catch different modes of transport.
- Move like a specific form of transport; e.g. a car, truck, bus. Follow the teacher's directions to create problems like traffic jams.
- Build models of cars, trucks or spacecraft using blocks or recycled materials.
- Mime scenes such as crossing the road, putting on a bicycle helmet or putting on a seatbelt in a car or aeroplane.
- Follow a procedure to make a paper plane, rocket or parachute.
- Plan some exercises for astronauts to do while sitting in their spacecraft.

Interpersonal

- Ask small groups of children to construct objects that travel by rolling. Supply everyday materials for them to use.
- In a group, discuss the 'best' forms of transport. List the advantages and disadvantages of each.
- In a group, create a television commercial for a form of transport.
- Work in a group to brainstorm and list types of transport.
- Work with a partner to make a list of rules for aircraft passengers.

Musical–Rhythmic

- Play recordings of transport noises and ask the children to identify them.
- Read rhyming poems about transport and then perform them.
- Sing transport songs like 'The wheels on the bus'. Change the lyrics to suit other forms of transport; e.g. 'The doors on the train'.
- Listen to music containing transport noises such as horns, screeching tyres or engines starting. Draw the images conjured up.
- Perform a musical item about transport; e.g. 'Row, row, row your boat' sung as a round.
- Listen to the song 'Those magnificent men in their flying machines'. Use percussion and actions to perform it.

Intrapersonal

- Write a story about your life as a bus, train etc.
- Choose an unusual form of transport and explain why it would be fun to travel this way.
- Research people who have had an impact on transport; e.g. Henry Ford, the Wright brothers.
- Investigate how transport at school or in the local community caters for people with disabilities.
- Write a report about the first moon landing.
- Explain which form of transport you think is the safest and why.
- Each child lists the types of public transport he/she thinks would best suit their community; e.g. trains, buses, ferries.

TRANSPORT
INFORMATIONAL TEXT

What is Transport?

What does the word 'transport' make you think of? Maybe a jet aeroplane full of hundreds of passengers, or catching a bus to go to school. Perhaps it makes you think of waiting for the postman to arrive with an exciting letter. Transport certainly makes our lives easier! Without transport, we could not travel to different places or get the things we want or need.

There have been some big changes to transport over the years. The first people had to walk everywhere. They carried or dragged the things they wanted to move around.

Later, people built things or used animals to help them travel from place to place more quickly or to carry things for them. These included wagons and boats as well as animals like donkeys and horses.

About 200 years ago, people invented forms of transport that use engines. Today, most of the types of transport we use have engines. This includes planes, cars, ships and spacecraft. We use a huge range of transport that takes us over the land, into the air and on or under the water.

Land Transport

There are many ways of travelling over the land. Some forms of land transport that don't use engines are walking and riding bikes or horses. In some countries, people use animals like camels, elephants and oxen to transport things.

There are many types of land transport that use engines—ranging from cars to snowmobiles! If you live in a city, you will see many different types of engine-powered land transport every day, like cars, buses, trains and trucks.

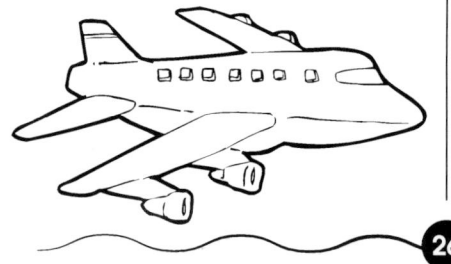

Air Transport

Feel like travelling through the sky? You might like to try something without an engine, like a hot air balloon or a hang-glider. These types of air transport are mostly used just for fun.

Would you prefer your air transport to have an engine? Most people do! Maybe you would like to fly in a helicopter. They are very easy to move around in the air, so they are often used to rescue people. But they would not win a race against a plane. Jet planes are the fastest type of plane. A big passenger jet can fly at least eight times faster than you would travel in a car on a motorway! Only spacecraft can travel faster than this.

MULTIPLE INTELLIGENCES

TRANSPORT
INFORMATIONAL TEXT

Water Transport

People all over the world use water transport without engines to travel on rivers, lakes and the sea. Some of these types of transport are canoes, kayaks and sailing boats. Some people even live on their water transport! These are called houseboats.

There are also many types of water transport that use engines. The biggest of these are ships. Ships are used to transport people as well as things we need. Things that are transported by ship are called 'cargo'.

How would you like to travel in a more unusual form of water transport? What about a hovercraft or a submarine? A hovercraft travels over the water on a cushion of air. This means it can also travel on land! A submarine travels underwater. Some submarines can stay underwater for months at a time without having to come up to the surface.

Transport Workers

Many people have jobs that involve transport. Some of these people drive or fly different forms of transport, like pilots, truck drivers and couriers. Other people help to keep transport working, like engineers and mechanics. There are also many other jobs in transport. Some of the jobs you may know are flight attendants, baggage handlers, conductors and travel agents.

Transport Problems

Even though transport that uses engines helps us to travel more quickly, it has also created problems for the environment. The exhaust fumes from some forms of transport, such as motor vehicles, pollute the air. This can harm the health of people, animals and plants. Cars also cause other problems, such as traffic jams and noise pollution. We can help to reduce these problems by sharing cars with other people, using public transport and riding a bike or walking instead of driving a car.

Some other problems caused by transport are oil spills by ships and chopping down trees to make way for new roads. Can you think of some ways we could try to solve these problems?

MULTIPLE INTELLIGENCES

The multiple intelligence focus for this activity is verbal–linguistic.

A verbal–linguistic child thinks in words.
He/She learns best through activities involving reading, writing and speaking.

Objective

- Writes a story plan for a creative narrative.

Preparation

- Provide extra paper for writing drafts/final copies of stories.
- Teachers could think of some unusual or fun forms of transport to suggest to the children. These might include inline skates, skateboards, submarines, hovercraft etc. Some pictures of these forms of transport could be shown to the children to act as a story stimulus.

Teacher information

- Before the children begin the worksheet, teachers should hold a class discussion about some suitable forms of transport the children could use for their stories.
- Teachers should ask for suggestions from the class for Questions 2 and 3. The teacher could allow time for the children to write their responses to each question before dealing with the next part.
- Before the children complete Question 4, teachers should allow them to write a draft on a separate sheet of paper.

Answers

Teacher check

Additional activities

- Read fantasy stories that contain unusual forms of transport—flying animals, broomsticks, flying carpets etc.
- Ask the children to design fantasy forms of transport they would like to try. (visual–spatial)

CURRICULUM LINKS			
England	Literacy	Yr2	• write sustained stories
Northern Ireland	English	KS 1	• write in a variety of forms, including stories
Republic of Ireland	English	1st/ 2nd	• write in a variety of genres, e.g. stories
Scotland	English	A	• show awareness of beginnings, middles and endings in imaginative writing
Wales	English	KS 1	• write in a range of forms, e.g. stories

A TRAVEL ADVENTURE!

Task — *You will plan a story about travelling to school in an unusual way.*

If you wrote a story about how you travel to school each day, it might not be very exciting. But imagine if you travelled by flying carpet or camel! Use these steps to help plan a story about travelling to school in an unusual way.

1 Tick one of the forms of transport below or write your own.

☐ *flying carpet*   ☐ *camel*   ☐ *racing car*   ☐ *hot air balloon*

_____

2 Think of a reason why you might need to use the transport you chose to get to school. For example, you go by camel because your family owns a herd of them.

_____

3 Write ideas for the beginning, middle and end of your story.

Beginning How does your story start? (You might unroll a flying carpet and say some magic words. Your mum might put a saddle on your camel.)

_____

_____

Middle What exciting things might happen on the way to school? (Perhaps your transport breaks down or you might rescue someone along the way.)

_____

_____

End What happens when you finally arrive at school? (You might land on the roof. Everyone might cheer you!)

_____

_____

4 Use your plan to write your story on a separate sheet of paper.

The multiple intelligence focus for this activity is logical–mathematical.

A logical–mathematical child thinks rationally and in abstractions.
He/She learns best through activities involving problem-solving, numbers and patterns.

Objectives

• Sorts forms of transport into air, land and water.

• Creates a simple pictogram from given data.

Preparation

• Depending on the class's experience, teachers may like to show and explain examples of pictograms.

Teacher information

• Before the children are given the worksheet, hold a class discussion about some of the forms of air, land and water transport. The children can then complete Questions 1 and 2.

• Ask the children to count the number of each type of transport they have listed. There should be three for 'Air', five for 'Land' and four for 'Water'. The children can then be instructed to cut out as many picture icons as they need from the bottom of the page to complete the pictogram. The children could colour the correct number of pictures they will need before they cut them out.

Answers

1. air – plane, hang glider

   land – car, bike, train, truck

   water – ship, canoe, jetski

2. Teacher check

3.

Forms of transport

	1	2	3	4	5
Air	☀ air	☀ air	☀ air		
Land	🚗 land	🚗 land	🚗 land	🚗 land	🚗 land
Water	🐟 water	🐟 water	🐟 water	🐟 water	

Note: Teacher check child choices

Additional activities

• Create a simple time line showing some of the advances in air transport.

• Use magazine pictures to create a class picture dictionary that shows different types of air, land and water transport. (verbal–linguistic)

CURRICULUM LINKS			
England	Numeracy	Yr 2	• solve a problem by sorting, classifying and organising information in simple ways, such as a pictogram
Northern Ireland	Maths	KS 1	• collect and record data, including simple pictograms
Republic of Ireland	Maths	1st/ 2nd	• represent, read and interpret pictograms
Scotland	Maths	A	• organise information by sorting into specific sets and display using pictures
Wales	Maths	KS 1	• sort and classify a set of objects and record data using range of charts

AIR, LAND OR WATER?

1 Write each form of transport in the correct box.

car   ship   plane   bike

train   canoe   truck   jetski   hang glider

Air	Land	Water

2 Add one more form of transport to each box.

3 Show the numbers of air, land and sea transport listed above by making a pictogram. Cut out and glue the pictures below onto your pictogram.

Forms of transport

	1	2	3	4	5
Air					
Land					
Water					

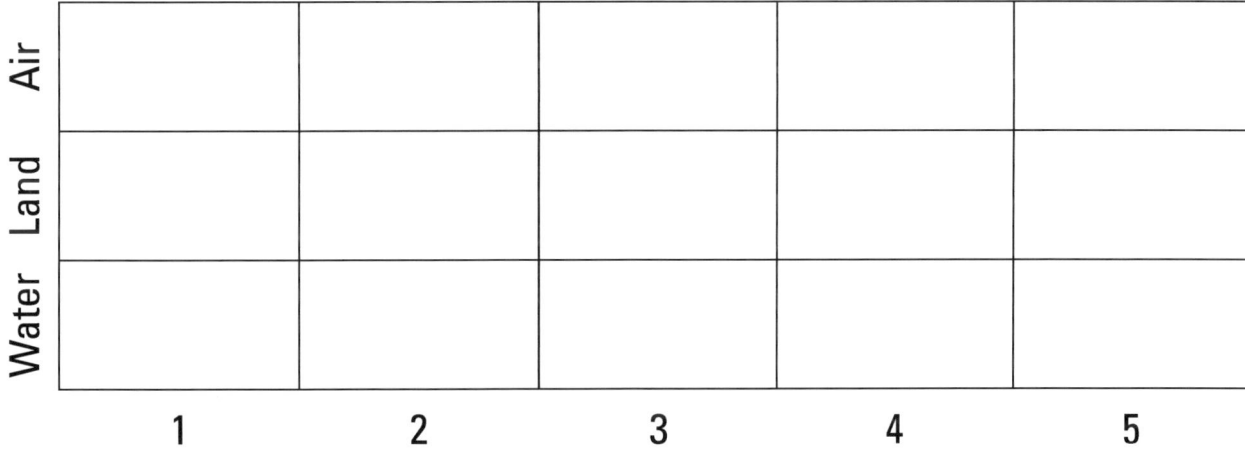

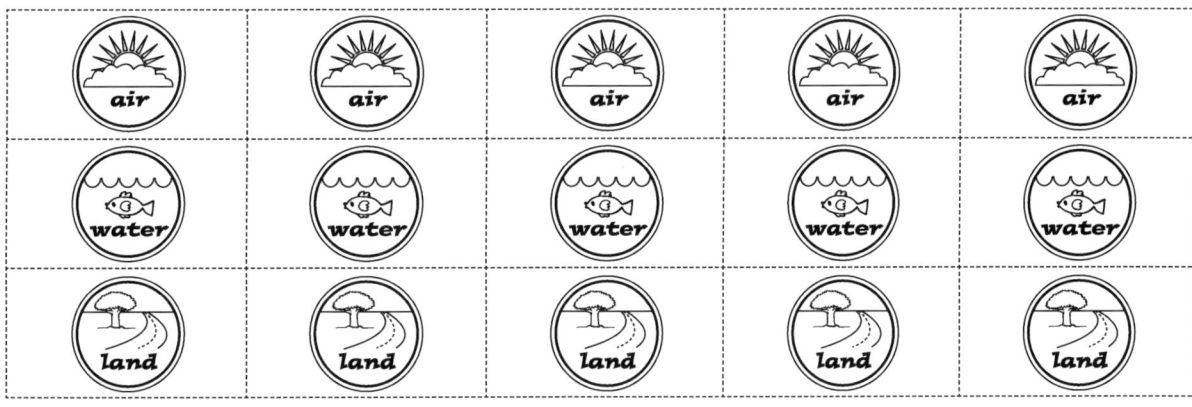

The multiple intelligence focus for this activity is naturalist.

A naturalist child has an awareness of the patterns in nature.
He/She learns best through activities involving animals, plants and the environment.

Objective

- Considers how people can help to reduce air pollution caused by transport.

Preparation

- Teachers may like to gather facts about the problems caused by air pollution or pictures of cities badly affected by air pollution to share with the children.

Teacher information

- Before giving the worksheet to the children, discuss the possible health problems that exhaust fumes from transport can cause; e.g. triggering asthma attacks. Some pictures of cities badly affected by air pollution could be shown; e.g. Athens. Ask the children to suggest some alternatives to using cars.

- Read the information text at the top of the page with the class and discuss if necessary. The children can then complete Question 1.

- Discuss the ideas the children wrote for Question 1.

- Discuss other problems caused by transport; e.g. noise pollution, road accidents and land clearing. The children can then complete Question 2.

- The children should work with partners to complete Question 3. When they have finished, the solutions they devised can be discussed with the class.

Answers

Teacher check

Additional activities

- Find out what cities, such as Athens, are doing to try reduce air pollution. (intrapersonal)

- Read about some of the environmentally-friendly cars that have been invented in recent years; e.g. air-powered cars. (verbal–linguistic)

CURRICULUM LINKS			
England	Science	KS 1	• care for the environment
Northern Ireland	Science	KS 1	• find out how human activities create a variety of waste products
Republic of Ireland	Science	1st/ 2nd	• identify and discuss simple strategies for improving and caring for the environment
Scotland	Science	C	• explain how the environment can be protected
Wales	PSE	KS 1	• be concerned about their environment

TRANSPORT PROBLEMS

Transport helps us in many ways but the exhaust fumes from some forms of transport pollute the air. This can harm the health of people, animals and plants. We can help to reduce air pollution by sharing cars with other people, using public transport and riding a bike or walking instead of driving a car.

1 Read each story below and then write some ways the people in each story could help to reduce air pollution.

(a) Anna and her brother, Corey, live two streets away from their school. Their mum drives them to school every day.

_____

_____

(b) Josh and Daniel live in the same village and work in the same office. Josh rides his motorbike to work each day. Daniel drives his car.

_____

_____

(c) Kira drives a long way to work at a hospital each day. Everyone she works with lives close to the hospital.

_____

_____

2 List some other problems transport can cause for people, animals or plants.

3 Discuss some solutions to these with a partner.

The multiple intelligence focus for this activity is visual–spatial.

> A visual–spatial child thinks in images, colours and shape.
> He/She learns best through activities involving visualisation.

Objective

- Designs a uniform for a ship's crew.

Preparation

- The children will require drawing materials such as crayons or coloured pencils.

- Teachers may like to collect pictures of ship or airline crew uniforms and company logos to show the children.

Teacher information

- Before giving the worksheet to the children, show some pictures of ship or airline crew uniforms. Discuss the colours and patterns and how comfortable the children think the clothes would be to wear.

- Read the information at the top of the sheet to the class. Ask the children to suggest what kinds of clothes are the most comfortable to wear (this may include types of materials as well as styles), what sort of clothing protects us from the sun and what colours or patterns are 'bright'. Teachers may also need to explain the term 'logo'. Some examples of real ship or airline logos could be shown.

- The children should complete Questions 1 and 2 individually. If required, teachers could ask some volunteers to share what they wrote for Question 1 with the class before Question 2 is completed. Teachers should also remind the children to draw an enlarged version of the hat logo in the circle given.

Answers

Teacher check

Additional activities

- Design some suitable uniforms for other types of transport workers. (visual–spatial)

CURRICULUM LINKS			
England	D & T	KS 1	• communicate ideas using a variety of methods, including drawing
Northern Ireland	Technology	KS 1	• respond to questions
Republic of Ireland	Science	1st/ 2nd	• clarify and communicate through pictures
Scotland	Technology	B	• make a simple plan by drawing
Wales	D & T	KS 1	• record ideas using pictures

CRUISE SHIP UNIFORM

Troppo Ships is a new company that will take people on island cruises. You have been asked to design a shirt, shorts and hat for the ship's crew. Here are some things you need to know.

- **The clothes must be comfortable and protect the crew from the sun.**
- **The clothes must have bright colours or patterns.**
- **The hat must have a logo that shows what the company does. For example, the logo might show an island.**

1 Write some ideas for your uniform design in the boxes below.

Shirt	Shorts	Hat/Logo

2 Draw your designs in the boxes below. Draw the logo for the hat in the circle so it can be seen easily.

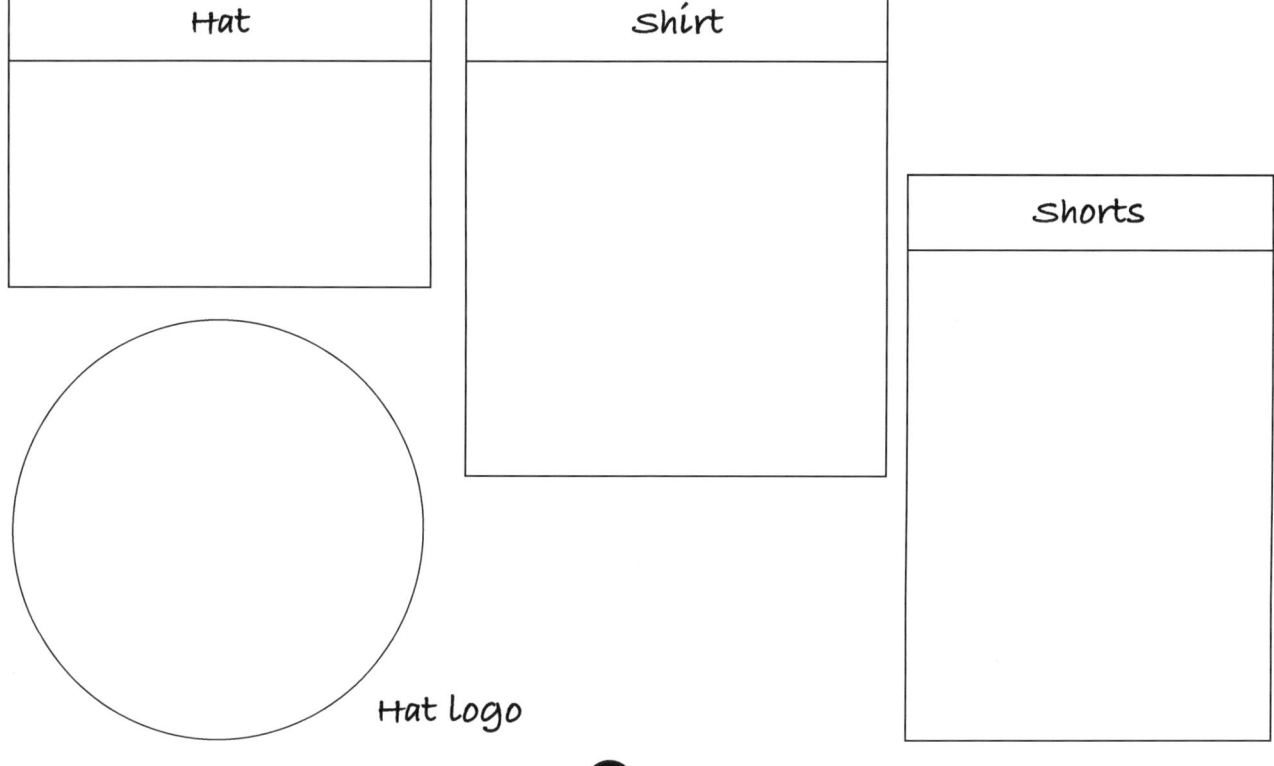

Hat

Shirt

Shorts

Hat logo

The multiple intelligence focus for this activity is bodily–kinaesthetic.

> A bodily–kinaesthetic child has good physical awareness.
> He/She learns best through 'hands-on' activities.

Objective

- Makes and modifies a paper helicopter.

Preparation

- It is suggested that classroom assistants and/or parent helpers are invited to the classroom to help the children with cutting out and modifying their helicopters. Note: As the focus of this lesson is bodily-kinaesthetic, the children should do as much of this activity on their own as possible.

- Each child will need a pair of scissors and at least three paperclips.

Teacher information

- Teachers should show the children how to cut out the pattern along the solid lines before they begin work. It is also suggested that teachers demonstrate each step of folding the helicopter before the children try themselves.

- The children can complete Question 2 individually or in small groups. They may require some help with the modifications suggested.

- The only modification that should have an effect on the helicopter will be adding paperclips to the base. These will cause the helicopter to spin faster to the ground.

Answers

Teacher check

Additional activities

- Make and test-fly paper aeroplanes.

- Challenge small groups of children to make models of different forms of transport using everyday materials; e.g. cars, boats.

CURRICULUM LINKS			
England	D & T	KS 1	• complete focused practical tasks that develop a range of skills and knowledge
Northern Ireland	Technology	KS 1	• develop manipulative skills and comment on what happened
Republic of Ireland	Science	1st/ 2nd	• make simple objects
Scotland	Technology	A	• use given resources and processes to carry out a task safely
Wales	D & T	KS 1	• talk about the ideas to solve the task in hand

MAKE A HELICOPTER

1 Make a paper helicopter by following the steps below.

(a) Cut along the solid lines of the pattern.

(b) Fold 'A' wing towards you.

(c) Fold 'B' wing away from you.

(d) Fold 'C' and 'D' so they overlap.

(e) Fold 'E' upwards along the dotted line.

2 Your helicopter is ready! Stand up and hold it above your head. Let it drop to the floor. How did it fly?

perfectly	okay	not so well	badly

3 Make some changes to your helicopter and drop it again. Write what happens.

• Add some paperclips to the bottom of the helicopter.

_____

• Fold 'E' over again so the helicopter is shorter.

_____

• Fold 'C' and 'D' over again so the helicopter is thinner.

_____

4 Circle the best change you made.

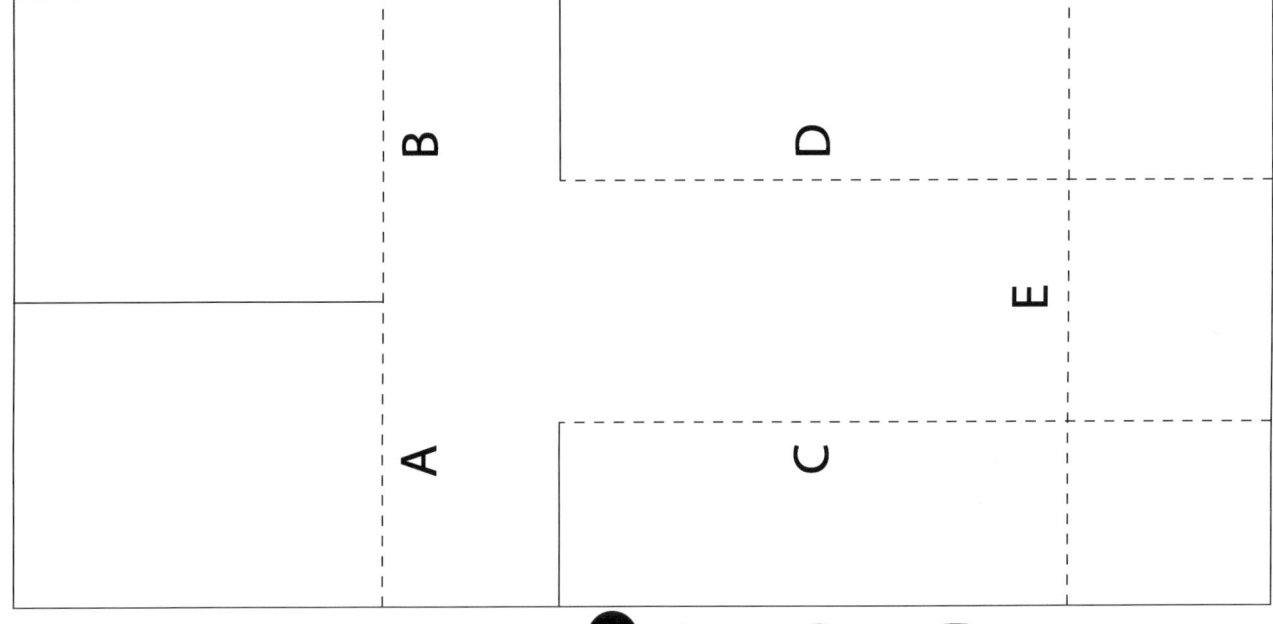

The multiple intelligence focus for this activity is musical–rhythmic.

A musical–rhythmic child has an awareness of music and sound.
He/She learns best through activities involving music or rhythms.

Objectives

- Creates a song based on a given tune.
- Performs a song with a partner.

Preparation

- The children will need to work with partners to complete most of Question 2 and Questions 3 and 4.
- The lyrics of 'The big jet plane' should be sung to the tune of 'The wheels on the bus'. Teachers should sing it a few times with the children until they seem confident with the tune.

Teacher information

- Before the children complete Question 2, teachers could ask the class to suggest suitable words for each form of transport. Encourage one-syllable words.
- For Questions 2 (b) and 2 (c), emphasise to the children that they need to decide on two forms of transport and three words for each. They should choose words from their partner's and their own lists.
- Before the children complete Question 2 (d), ask the class for suggestions of other appropriate last lines that fit the song's rhythm.
- Allow the children 10 – 15 minutes to practise their songs. The class could suggest some appropriate movements for different forms of transport before the partners begin practising.
- The songs may be performed for the class or a small group.

Answers

Teacher check

Additional activities

- Make up rhythmic chants to represent different forms of transport.

CURRICULUM LINKS			
England	Music	KS 1	• use voices expressively by singing songs and rehearsing and performing for others
Northern Ireland	Music	KS 1	• join in singing rhymes and simple songs
Republic of Ireland	Music	1st/ 2nd	• sing with increasing vocal control and confidence
Scotland	Music	A	• sing action songs
Wales	Music	KS 1	• sing a variety of simple songs

TUNEFUL TRANSPORT

You will create and perform songs about transport.

1 Sing this song with your teacher.

The big jet plane goes zoom, whoosh, roar.
Zoom, whoosh, roar
Zoom, whoosh, roar.
The big jet plane goes zoom, whoosh, roar.
Way up in the sky.

2 Write your own transport songs by following the steps below.

(a) List words that describe the noises these forms of transport make; for example, 'whoosh', 'clank', 'bang', 'toot'.

train _____

truck _____

bike _____

bus _____

speedboat _____

(b) Find a partner. Choose two of the forms of transport.

(c) Circle three 'noisy' words you both like for these two forms of transport. The words should come from both of your lists.

(d) Use the tune of 'The big jet plane' to create two songs with your partner about the two forms of transport. You will need to think up the last line for each song; for example, 'Down there on the road'.

Write the two last lines you thought up.

Song 1: _____

Song 2: _____

3 Practise the songs with your partner. You can add movement to make them more exciting!

4 When you have finished practising, perform your songs for the class.

The multiple intelligence focus for this activity is interpersonal.

An interpersonal child enjoys being in groups or teams.
He/She learns best through activities involving working with others.

Objectives

- Works in a group to compose interview questions.
- Conducts an interview as part of a group.

Preparation

- Arrange a number of transport workers to be interviewed by the class. They may include pilots, mechanics, bus drivers, baggage handlers, flight attendants or travel agents. Explain to each person that they will be interviewed by three children who will ask him/her two questions each about his/her work. Ask each transport worker to keep his/her answers short, as the children will need to write the answer as they hear it.
- The children will need to work in groups of three.

Teacher information

- Discuss the concept of an interview with the class. Ask for some ideas for questions to ask transport workers about their jobs. The questions should cover duties and routines and feelings about their work.
- Allocate a transport worker to each group and ask each child to write the title of his/her job in the space provided.
- Groups of children brainstorm ideas for Question 1. Each group could then share some of their ideas with the class.
- Before the groups begin Question 2, discuss the problems that might occur in deciding which six questions to choose. The children could suggest some ways their groups could choose questions that make everyone in their group happy; e.g. have everyone in the group choose at least one question each. The groups can use similar strategies to complete Question 3.
- Set up the interviewees in a quiet space with their group. The children should take it in turns to ask one question at a time. Instruct the children to write the transport worker's answer in notes when they have finished speaking. The other members of the group should refrain from asking the next question until the child has finished writing.
- For Question 5, ask the groups to report the answers to the class. Each group member should report the answers to the two questions he/she asked.

Answers

Teacher check

Additional activities

- Role-play different transport occupations in small groups. (bodily–kinaesthetic)
- Complete transport occupation profiles for different transport workers. Some research may be needed. (verbal–linguistic)
- Conduct an excursion to an airport and use as a stimulus for writing activities. (bodily–kinaesthetic)

CURRICULUM LINKS			
England	English	KS 1	• speak to different people, including other adults
Northern Ireland	English	KS 1	• take turns at talking and listening
Republic of Ireland	English	1st/ 2nd	• engage in real situations involving language use
Scotland	English	C	• select questions appropriate to the purpose of an interview and interview visitors to the school
Wales	English	KS 1	• talk to different audiences, including other adults

TRANSPORT WORKER INTERVIEW

Task *You will work in a group to write some questions to ask a transport worker and interview a transport worker with a group.*

1 In a group of three, brainstorm some questions you would like to ask a transport worker about his/her job. Write the group's ideas in the space below.

Our transport worker's job is: _____

2 Choose six questions that everyone in the group likes. Write them below.

- _____

- _____

- _____

- _____

- _____

- _____

3 Decide who will ask the transport worker each question. Each member of your group must ask two questions. Circle the two questions you will ask.

4 As a group, interview the transport worker. Write the answers to your two questions in the boxes below.

5 With your group, report the transport worker's answers to the class.

The multiple intelligence focus for this activity is intrapersonal.

An intrapersonal child understands and analyses his/her thoughts and feelings.
He/She learns best through individual activities.

Objective

- Researches an unusual form of transport.

Preparation

- Teachers should collect nonfiction books about unusual or fun forms of transport; e.g. surfboards, hovercraft, hot air balloons, skateboards, inline skates, pogo sticks etc. Check that the books contain information about the history of the transport and labelled pictures.

- The children will require drawing materials to complete Question 2 (e).

Teacher information

- Read Question 1 with the children, then show them the books that have been collected. The books could be displayed on desks at the front of the classroom. To avoid conflict, a few children at a time could come to choose a book.

- The children must complete Question 2 individually. For Question 2 (e), they may copy a labelled illustration from the book they are using or draw their own picture based on an illustration in the book and add an appropriate label.

- When the worksheet has been completed, some children may like to share their answers with the class.

Answers

Teacher check

Additional activities

- Write reports based on the information written on the worksheets. (verbal–linguistic)

- Children design a form of transport they think may be invented in the future. Explain how it works. (intrapersonal)

CURRICULUM LINKS			
England	Literacy	Yr 1	• read non-fiction books and select information needed
Northern Ireland	English	KS 1	• read information books for writing tasks and collect information relevant to specific purposes
Republic of Ireland	English	1st/ 2nd	• engage with a wide variety of text and perform simple information retrieval tasks
Scotland	English	B	• use a wide selection of informational and reference texts
Wales	English	KS 1	• read information and make use of a range of sources of information

TRANSPORT RESEARCH

self wise

1 Find at least one nonfiction book about a fun or unusual form of transport. It can be one of the forms of transport below or you can choose your own.

surfboard

hovercraft

hot-air balloon

2 Use your book(s) to answer these questions.

(a) When and where was this form of transport first used or invented?

_____

_____

(b) List some changes that have happened since it was first used or invented.

_____

_____

(c) Name a person who is described in your book. What does he/she have to do with your form of transport?

_____

_____

(d) Write two more interesting facts about your form of transport.

_____

_____

_____

_____

(e) Use the information in your book to draw a picture of your form of transport. Add a label.

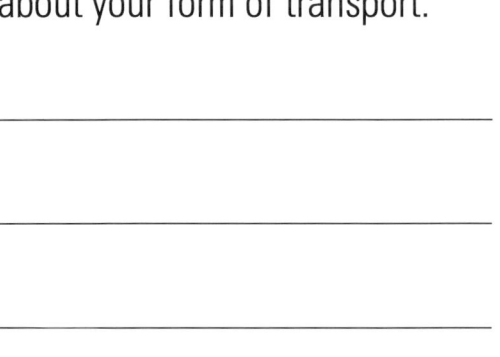

MULTIPLE INTELLIGENCES

TRANSPORT – MY SELF-ASSESSMENT

After completing this unit, I was able to ...

word wise	plan a story about travelling to school in an unusual way.	☆ ☆ ☆ ☆ ☆
logic wise	sort forms of transport into air, land and water and make a pictogram.	☆ ☆ ☆ ☆ ☆
nature wise	consider how people can help reduce air pollution caused by transport.	☆ ☆ ☆ ☆ ☆
picture wise	design a uniform for a ship's crew.	☆ ☆ ☆ ☆ ☆
body wise	make and test a paper helicopter.	☆ ☆ ☆ ☆ ☆
music wise	create and perform songs about transport.	☆ ☆ ☆ ☆ ☆
people wise	work in a group to write some questions to ask a transport worker and interview the worker with a group.	☆ ☆ ☆ ☆ ☆
self wise	research an unusual form of transport.	☆ ☆ ☆ ☆ ☆

What I learnt

THE SEA

Informational text ┄┄┄┄ ☐   ☐ ┄┄┄┄ Beach drama

word wise
Sea creature ┄┄┄┄ ☐   ☐ ┄┄┄┄ Rounds of the sea
music wise

logic wise
Underwater grid ┄┄┄┄ ☐   ☐ ┄┄┄┄ Shipwrecks
people wise

nature wise
Endangered sea life ┄┄┄┄ ☐   ☐ ┄┄┄┄ Message in a bottle
self wise

picture wise
Underwater diorama ┄┄┄┄ ☐   ☐ ┄┄┄┄ My self-assessment

What I know	What I want to know

Keywords

Name:	Date:

THE SEA OVERVIEW

Verbal–Linguistic

- Read factual information about plants and animals which live under the sea and write a report about one.
- Write a story about a visit to the beach.
- Learn and say rhymes and poems about the sea.
- Write a diary about: 'A day in the life of _____ living underwater'.
- Play barrier games involving underwater scenes.
- Create a class A-Z or alphabet search of sea creatures.
- Write 'What am I? puzzles about sea creatures.
- Write a description of a sea creature.
- Write five questions which have the answer, 'the sea'.
- Write a legend; e.g. 'Why is the sea salty?'
- Give a talk about shells, tidal waves etc.
- Write a poem about a favourite sea creature.
- Study sea myths and legends; e.g. mermaids, the kraken.
- Read books about sea creatures; e.g. *The Rainbow Fish* and complete a book review.

Naturalist

- Visit the sea to observe, record and collect seashells, sea creatures etc.
- Explore a rock pool at the beach.
- Collect and bring objects found at the beach to display on a nature table.
- List the characteristics of a sea creature or plant.
- Discuss the impact of whale hunting on specific species.
- Set up a class aquarium.
- Keep hermit crabs as class pets.
- Research differences between saltwater and freshwater crocodiles.
- Discuss differences between dolphins and sharks.
- Compare sea and land plants.
- Compare sea and land mammals.

Logical–Mathematical

- Compare the lengths or weights of different sea creatures.
- Count the number of different kinds of sea creatures in a picture. Say if groups have more, less or the same numbers.
- Collect data about specific sea creatures.
- Investigate types of sea transport and uses and classify into groups.
- Locate the main oceans and seas on a world map.
- Categorise sea creatures.
- Tally sea creatures and graph results.
- Sort pictures of old and new ways to travel by sea and label.
- Sort items found or used at the beach into living and non-living.

Visual–Spatial

- View excerpts of films or documentaries about the sea; e.g. *Finding Nemo,* or *The little mermaid* and ask children to draw a favourite scene or character.
- Create a class mural of a coral reef.
- Design a strange sea creature.
- Create a sea jigsaw.
- Use crayon resist to create an underwater scene.
- Use a fishing net to display sea objects and art.
- Create a wanted or warning poster about a dangerous sea creature.
- Create a collage of sea creatures on an underwater picture.
- Draw a picture titled 'At the beach'.
- Construct a diorama of an ideal environment for a sea creature.
- Trace around a child and make a life-size collage of a 'sun-smart' beach-goer.
- Design a costume to wear to a sea theme party.

THE SEA OVERVIEW

Bodily–Kinaesthetic

- Small groups of children use streamers and move to show the different moods of the sea; e.g. choppy, calm, rough.
- Perform plays of sea myths or legends; e.g. King Neptune
- Make a mobile to show things under the sea; e.g. twisted paper strips for seaweed.
- Paint the classroom windows blue and make sea creatures to hang around the room to create an underwater wonderland.
- Build sandcastles or sand creatures at the beach or in a sandpit.
- Choreograph a sea creature dance to appropriate music.
- Hold sea creatures sports; e.g. crab races.
- Mirror movement made by a partner representing the sea.
- Follow a recipe to cook a seafood dish.
- Use human sculptures to create a sea table.
- Mime eel or shark movements.

Interpersonal

- Small groups of children plan a party with a sea theme. They can decide on appropriate decorations, food, invitations etc.
- In pairs, children interview each other about his/her life as a sea creature; e.g. whale, stingray.
- Form teams to play games using team names related to the sea.
- In small groups, plan and make a poster about caring for the sea; e.g. 'No rubbish overboard'.
- Plan an excursion to the beach in groups. Decide time, place, transport, food and activities.
- Research products from the sea and fish skins; e.g. jewellery, fish, shellfish, salt, seaweed, ornaments.
- In groups, research people whose work involves the sea.

Musical–Rhythmic

- Learn and sing songs about the sea.
- Use percussion instruments to accompany sea songs.
- Learn rhymes and jingles about the sea.
- Listen to ocean sounds (waves, gentle/pounding).
- Use hands to show how sea creatures move.
- Use a shell as a stimulus for creating sea music.
- Listen to whale and dolphin sounds. Ask children to describe how the sounds make them feel.
- Invite guest musicians to play music with a sea theme.
- Listen to *The yellow submarine* and ask children to add appropriate sound effects.

Intrapersonal

- Write a report about a sea creature.
- Read fiction and nonfiction sea books about the sea and write a book review on one.
- Draw a picture of a sea creature described in a book.
- Learn about the life cycles of various sea creatures.
- Reflect on personal feelings and actions if lost at sea and beyond the sight of land.
- Create a pamphlet that describes what people could do to save a particular endangered sea creature.
- Write a list of safety rules for the beach.
- Compare ships of the past and the present.
- Research to find out how submarines descend and ascend.

THE SEA
INFORMATIONAL TEXT
The oceans

When we go to the beach for a swim or even sail on the oceans, it is difficult to understand just how big they are.

The Pacific, Atlantic, Indian, Arctic and Antarctic oceans cover more than 70 per cent of the Earth's surface. Some parts are quite shallow, but some areas are more than 10 kilometres deep. There are some underwater mountains much taller than Mount Everest, which is the tallest land mountain.

Endangered sea life

There are many species of sea creatures that may not survive. Read about some of them.

Sea creatures

The oceans are home to a giant number of different species of sea creatures from huge whales to the smallest plankton.

Leafy sea dragon

Leafy sea dragons are very rare. They only live in waters around South Australia and Western Australia. They belong to the same family as seahorses, but have leaflike parts which help them to hide in seaweed. They swim gracefully through the water using fins on their heads to steer. Leafy sea dragons eat plankton and sea lice. They are endangered mainly because of water pollution.

Dugong

Dugongs are grey, slow-moving mammals. It is thought that early sailors mistook them for mermaids. Dugongs live along the northern coastline of Australia and in the warm shallow waters of the Pacific and Indian oceans. They are sometimes called 'sea cows' because they eat seagrasses. Dugongs are endangered because seagrasses are being destroyed, and they are being attacked by killer whales, crocodiles and sharks.

Blue whale

The blue whale is the largest animal that has ever lived on earth. Blue whales can grow to about 25 metres long with a heart the size of a small car. Their call is louder than a jet engine. Blue whales eat plankton and krill (mini-prawns). They live in families called pods. They are found in all the oceans of the world. Blue whales were hunted for many years for their meat and oil. Now this is not happening as often, there is hope they will not always be endangered.

THE SEA
INFORMATIONAL TEXT
Dangers of the sea

The sea can change very quickly from beautiful calm, blue water to the huge grey waves and roaring wind of terrible storms crashing onto a rocky coast.

For ships and sailors, the sea has often been a very dangerous place. There are many interesting stories about well known shipwrecks like the *Amity II* that you can find out about.

The wreck of the Amity II

The sailing ship *Amity II* set sail from Melbourne, Australia, in May 1866, bound for England. Most of the passengers were successful prospectors returning home with their gold. On the seventh night the wind dropped and the clipper was surrounded by thick fog. When the fog lifted, the wind and seas began to toss the ship sideways. The lookout shouted 'land dead ahead'. The ship had drifted very close to the cliffs of an unknown land and was sent crashing onto rocks. The waves smashed the ship again and again along the cliff face and then suddenly it grew very dark. Because the ship had been swept inside a huge cave, some passengers and crew jumped into the water. Others lowered lifeboats, but only one of them reached the entrance to the cave. There were only 15 survivors.

The exhausted men and one woman rowed along the cliffs and finally found a safe place to land. They found an abandoned hut and fresh water. The captain guessed that they were on one of the Auckland Islands, south of New Zealand.

After many weeks they sent the lifeboat with four men towards New Zealand for help. Finally, in November, a ship was seen and they were saved.

In 1870 a survivor returned to search for the gold. He found the cave but not the missing gold. He reported seeing a hazy ghost ship appear and then vanish into the cave.

The multiple intelligence focus for this activity is verbal–linguistic.

A verbal–linguistic child thinks in words.
He/She learns best through activities involving reading, writing and speaking.

Objective

- Uses words associated with the sea to complete a wordsearch and to solve 'What am I?' puzzles.

Preparation

- Children will need coloured pencils to complete the wordsearch.
- Ensure that children can read and understand the 'sea' words.

Teacher information

- The wordsearch uses the words vertically and horizontally.
- After completing this page, encourage children to create their own wordsearch for other class members, using 10 words.

Answers

1 (a)

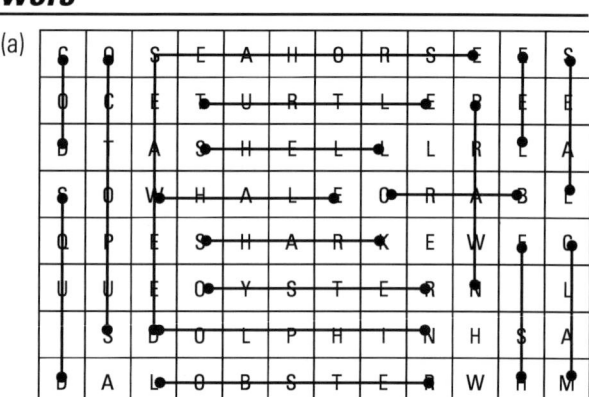

(b)   a, l, e, h, w

(c)   whale

2. (a)   turtle

(b)   oyster

(c)   shark

(d)   seahorse

Additional activities

- Write the wordsearch words in alphabetical order.
- Prepare a 'wanted' poster with a description and illustration of a missing sea animal (visual–spatial)
- Write five sentences each using both the 'sea' and the 'see' words correctly.

CURRICULUM LINKS			
England	Literacy	Yr 1/2	• encounter new words from shared experiences
Northern Ireland	English	KS 1	• build up a sight vocabulary
Republic of Ireland	English	1st/ 2nd	• build up a sight vocabulary of words from personal experience
Scotland	English	A	• use word banks
Wales	English	KS 1	• develop a vocabulary of words recognised and understood automatically and quickly

SEA CREATURE WORDSEARCH

Task — *You will complete a wordsearch using 'sea' words and use some of these words to answer 'What am I?' questions.*

1 (a) Find and colour the sea words in the wordsearch.

SEA WORDS

C	O	S	E	A	H	O	R	S	E	E	S
O	C	E	T	U	R	T	L	E	P	E	E
D	T	A	S	H	E	L	L	L	R	L	A
S	O	W	H	A	L	E	C	R	A	B	L
Q	P	E	S	H	A	R	K	E	W	F	C
U	U	E	O	Y	S	T	E	R	N	I	L
I	S	D	O	L	P	H	I	N	H	S	A
D	A	L	O	B	S	T	E	R	W	H	M

dolphin
octopus
seaweed
lobster
seahorse
squid
oyster
prawn
turtle
crab
fish
seal
cod
eel
whale
shell
clam
shark

(b) Write the five letters you didn't use in the wordsearch.

_____

(c) Unjumble the five letters to make the word in this sentence.

A __ __ __ __ __ *is a large sea mammal.*

2 Who am I?

Use a word from the wordsearch to solve these puzzles.

(a) I have flipper and a hard shell. I am a _____.	(b) I grow in a beautiful shell and sometimes there is a pearl with me. I am an _____.
(c) I have sharp teeth and many people are frightened of me. I am a _____.	(d) I have a curly tail and I hold my body up tall when I swim. I am a _____.

MULTIPLE INTELLIGENCES

The multiple intelligence focus for this activity is logical–mathematical.

A logical–mathematical child thinks rationally and in abstractions.
He/She learns best through activities involving problem-solving, numbers and patterns.

Objective

- Uses grid squares to locate and draw sea creatures.

Preparation

- Children need to be familiar with grid coordinates and to practise finding specified squares.

Teacher information

- Some children may find it difficult to locate grid squares. It may be helpful to allow them to use a ruler or to work with a partner, each following one of the coordinates.

- Children may enjoy colouring the sea creatures on their grids.

- Question 5: Some children may need assistance. Encourage them to use Questions 1–4 as a guide.

Answers

1. (a) 5
   (b) turtle
   (c) no
   (d) no
2–5. Teacher check

Additional activities

- Make a grid puzzle about the beach with questions and instructions for others to do. Work in small groups.

- Use a treasure map as a basis for grid points.

- Compile a list of sea creatures and classify as molluscs, fish, mammals or crustaceans. (verbal–linguistic)

CURRICULUM LINKS			
England	Numeracy	Yr 3	• find the position of a square on a grid of squares with the rows and columns labelled
Northern Ireland	Geography	KS 1	• use positional language to aid location
Republic of Ireland	Maths	1st/ 2nd	• follow simple directions, e.g. grids
Scotland	Maths	B	• use grid references to read or plot location on grid
Wales	Geography	KS 1	• use simple co-ordinates

UNDERWATER GRID

Task *You will use the grid squares to find and draw sea creatures.*

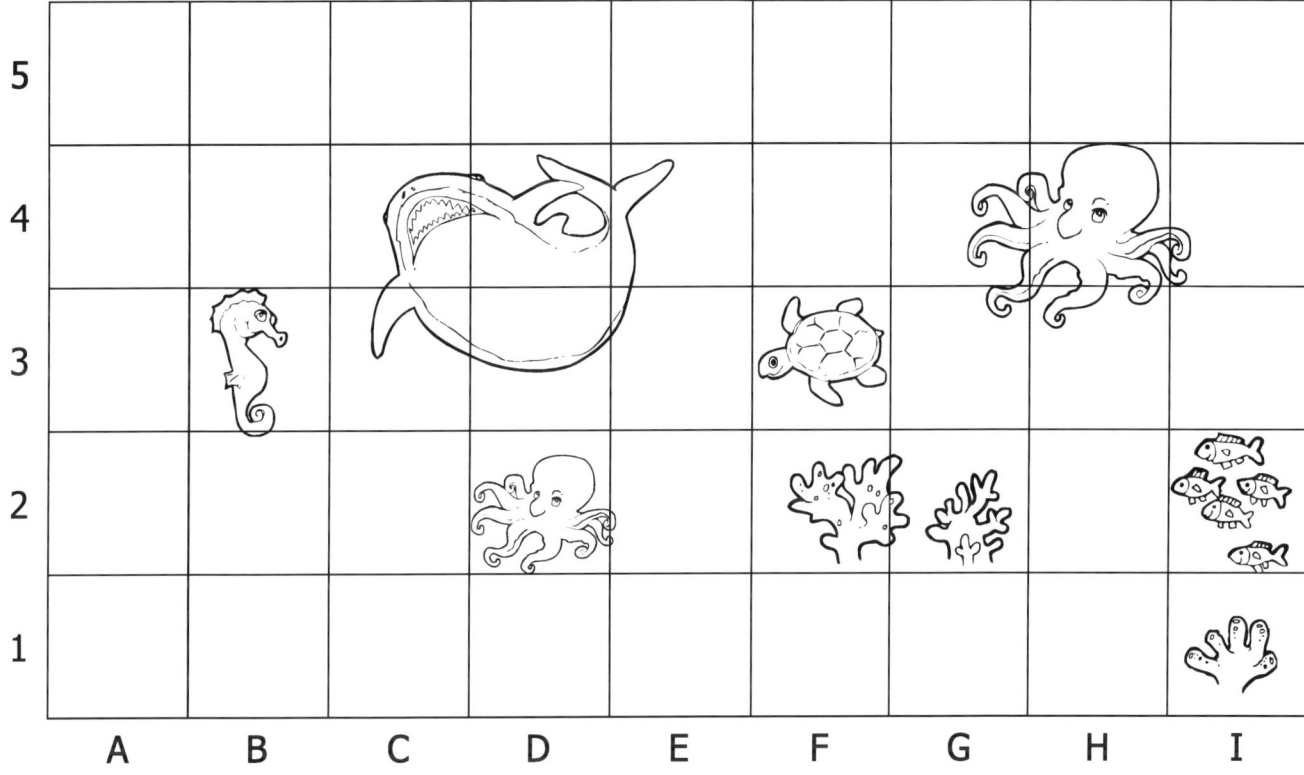

❶ (a) How many fish in (**I, 2**)?

_____

(b) What is in (**F, 3**)?

_____

(c) Is the shark in (**B, 3**)?

(**yes**)   (**no**)

(d) Is the bigger octopus in (**D, 2**)?

(**yes**)   (**no**)

❷ Draw a sea snake with its head in (**A, 4**) and its tail in (**G, 1**).

❸ Draw a fish in (**C, 5**), (**A, 1**), (**H, 1**) and (**E, 5**).

❹ Draw a starfish in: (**B, 1**), (**E, 2**), (**G, 5**) and (**C, 2**).

❺ Write a question on a separate page for a friend to answer.

The multiple intelligence focus for this activity is naturalist.

> A naturalist child has an awareness of the patterns in nature.
> He/She learns best through activities involving animals, plants and the environment.

Objective

- Researches information about endangered sea life to complete an information chart.

Preparation

- Discuss reasons why some sea life is endangered, including pollution from different sources, destruction of food sources, hunting and increasing numbers of predators.

Teacher information

- Encourage children to research information about endangered sea creatures and to complete a class list.

- Children then select some species to gather further information about.

- Refer children to informational text, page 48, where there are details about endangered sea creatures such as the leafy sea dragon, dugong and blue whale.

Answers

Teacher check

Additional activities

- Discuss conservation issues such as pollution and hunting.

- Discuss how oil spills affect sea life.

- Draw simple food chains and discuss what would happen if part of a chain is broken.

CURRICULUM LINKS			
England	Literacy	Yr 1	• read non-fiction books and select information needed
Northern Ireland	English	KS 1	• read information books for writing tasks and collect information relevant to specific purposes
Republic of Ireland	English	1st/ 2nd	• engage with a wide variety of text and perform simple information retrieval tasks
Scotland	English	B	• use a wide selection of informational and reference texts
Wales	English	KS 1	• read information and make use of a range of sources of information

ENDANGERED SEA LIFE

Task

You will find out about endangered sea life and complete an information chart.

Sea creature Picture and name	Where does it live and what does it eat?	Why is it endangered and can it be saved?
❶		
❷		
❸		

The multiple intelligence focus for this activity is visual–spatial.

> A visual–spatial child thinks in images, colours and shape.
> He/She learns best through activities involving visualisation.

Objective

- Creates an underwater diorama.

Preparation

- Discuss the different animals and plants to be found underwater.

- Children will need an empty shoe box, cellophane paper (clear – blue or green), cardboard, paint and crayons, string, scissors, sand, pebbles, small shells, glue and plasticine.

- Ask children to consider the size of their shoe box and to plan what will fit in it.

Teacher information

- A diorama is a three-dimensional model, usually made in a shoe box on its side. To represent an underwater scene, the children can decorate the inside of the box using paint, cellophane paper, sand, pebbles, shells etc. They can add extra detail by using appropriate plant and animal shapes. Objects are to be hung from the 'roof' of the shoe box and popped up from the bottom of the box to create a 3-D effect.

- Children need to be aware that objects inside the box will need to be clear and brightly coloured because they will be viewed through the cellophane paper.

Answers

Teacher check

Additional activities

- Create a mobile of sea creatures.

- Make pottery or papier-mâché sea creatures.

- Create a cartoon using sea creatures.

CURRICULUM LINKS			
England	Art & design	KS 1	• represent observations, make images and complete projects in three dimensions
Northern Ireland	Art & design	KS 1	• make three-dimensional structures by assembling, arranging and joining a variety of materials
Republic of Ireland	Visual arts	1st/ 2nd	• make imaginative structures
Scotland	Art & design	A	• construct 3-dimensional work with simple materials
Wales	Art	KS 1	• make objects in three dimensions for a variety of purposes using a range of materials

UNDERWATER DIORAMA

Task — *You will create an underwater diorama.*

Read the instructions and make a diorama.

1 Paint the inside of a shoe box blue.

2 Make the sea floor. Glue sand, pebbles and shells on to one side of the box.

3 Draw and paint brightly coloured seaweed and coral on the back wall.

4 Attach string to coloured cut-out sea creatures and hang them from the top of the box.

5 Make some plasticine sea creatures to sit in the sand.

6 Cover the front of the box with cellophane paper using glue or sticky tape.

Ideas for sea creatures

Colour, glue on cardboard and cut out.

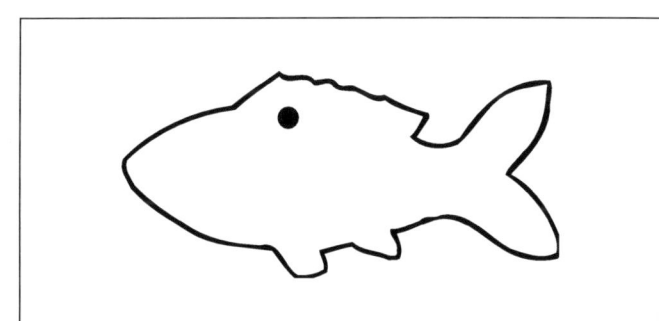

Draw two of your own.

The multiple intelligence focus for this activity is bodily–kinaesthetic.

A bodily–kinaesthetic child has good physical awareness. He/She learns best through 'hands-on' activities.

Objectives

- Role-plays animals and people at the beach.
- Creates and performs two short plays with a partner.

Preparation

- Children watch the way fish and or other sea creatures move; e.g. fish in an aquarium, a film such as *Finding Nemo*.
- Provide opportunities for children to visualise different sea creatures. Direct them to imagine how they would move body parts such as eyes, mouths, skin, tails and fins. Practise the movements.

Teacher information

- Children may benefit from discussing ways of working well with a partner.

  For example:
  - Listening to all ideas
  - Thinking of ways to improve performance
  - Making positive comments
  - Showing respect

- Allow groups to choose their best role-play to perform for the class. Ask the class to identify it and take turns to make positive comments starting with … 'I liked the way you …'

- Costume ideas:
  - *Octopus*
    Stuff stocking legs with newspaper and attach to a piece of wool to tie around children's chests.
  - *Turtle*
    Cut a large piece of card into a shell shape for the child's back. Decorate and attach with wool.
  - *Fish*
    Paper bag fish can be made by folding in the corners of the bottom of a paper bag and stapling it to form a fish's head. Stuff the bag with newspaper and close the end with a rubber band. Slide the rubber band up and fan out the end to make a tail. Decorate the fish.

Answers

Teacher check

Additional activities

- Role-play dangerous situations that occur at the beach.
- Create a poster warning of a beach danger. (visual-spatial)
- Plan exercises that sailors on a small ship could do at sea to keep fit and stretch all their muscles.

CURRICULUM LINKS			
England	English	KS 1	• create and sustain roles individually and when working with others
Northern Ireland	English	KS 1	• take part in drama activities, including role-play
Republic of Ireland	Drama	1st/ 2nd	• re-enact for others a scene that has been made in small-group work
Scotland	Drama	B	• sustain and develop a role and participate in small-scale presentations
Wales	English	KS 1	• participate in drama activities, improvisation and performances of varying kinds

BEACH DRAMA

body wise

1. Working with a partner, try to use all of your body, including your face, to show these actions.

Animals	People
• Flying fish twisting and flipping in and out of the water.	• Someone fishing with something big on the end of the line.
• Octopuses stretching and feeling their way across the sea floor.	• Children jumping and splashing in shallow water at the beach.
• Turtles swimming and gliding through the water.	• Two sailors in a yacht during a storm.
• Fish swimming around searching for food on the seabed.	• A child with a crab holding onto his or her big toe.

2 (a) Read the beginnings of these two short plays with a partner, then work out an ending for each.

(b) Perform your plays for the class.

At the beach	
PLAY ONE	**PLAY TWO**
A: Oh no! What is that?	**A:** You haven't got any suntan lotion on.
B: I don't know, but it feels really heavy. Help me!	**B:** It doesn't matter. It's really not very hot at the beach today.

The multiple intelligence focus for this activity is musical–rhythmic.

> A musical–rhythmic child has an awareness of music and sound.
> He/She learns best through activities involving music or rhythms.

Objective

- Learns to sing songs of the sea as rounds and uses text innovation to compose a similar song to sing as a round.

Preparation

- Discuss reasons why sailors often sang songs while at sea; for example, to fill long hours, or make tasks like pulling in ropes and scrubbing desks easier to endure.

Teacher information

- The rounds can be sung in two or four parts.
- Children need to know the words and rhythm well before attempting to sing it as a round.
- Before attempting to compose a song of their own:
  - Brainstorm verbs connected with the sea they may like to use; e.g. fishing, swimming, diving, playing.
  - Identify the rhyming words in the songs.
  - Identify the beat
    4 | | | |
    4 | | | •
    4 | | | |
    4 | | | •

Answers

None required

Additional activities

- Devise appropriate movements to mime for the different parts of the rounds. (bodily–kinaesthetic)
- Learn and sing sea songs such as 'Yellow submarine' or 'One day I went to sea', and add some sound effects.

CURRICULUM LINKS			
England	Music	KS 1	• use voices expressively by singing songs and rehearsing and performing for others
Northern Ireland	Music	KS 1	• join in singing rhymes and simple songs
Republic of Ireland	Music	1st/ 2nd	• sing with increasing vocal control and confidence
Scotland	Music	A	• sing action songs
Wales	Music	KS 1	• sing a variety of simple songs

ROUNDS OF THE SEA

music wise

Task • *You will learn to sing rounds about the sea and compose one of your own.*

1 Sailors often sing songs about the sea. Learn and enjoy these sea songs. When you know them well, sing them as rounds.

Row, row, row your boat,
Gently down the stream.
Merrily, merrily, merrily, merrily,
Life is but a dream.

Surf, surf, surf the waves,
Towards the hard white sand.
Splashing, splashing, splashing, splashing
Going into land.

Sail, sail, sail your boat,
Across the open sea.
Gliding, gliding, gliding, gliding,
Sailing is for me.

2 Write a similar sea song that you and your class can have fun singing as a round.

The multiple intelligence focus for this activity is interpersonal.

> An interpersonal child enjoys being in groups or teams.
> He/She learns best through activities involving working with others.

Objective

- Works in a groups to research and record information about a shipwreck.

Teacher information

- Discuss lighthouses – why they were built and where, why they were so tall and why lighthouse keepers lived a hard, lonely life. (such as isolation, location, harsh environment, poor weather, climbing up the stairs).

- Dangers to ships include storms, waves, wind, lightning, poor visibility, rocks, reefs, disease, mutiny, food, water, pirates, icebergs, mechanical and structural failure.

- Refer children to the Informational text, page 49, where the wreck of the *Amity II* is described.

Answers

Teacher check

Additional activities

- Work in a group to design and make a boat that floats.

- Discuss pirates with a small group. Work out ways of recording this information and plan an interesting presentation for the class.

- Design a poster offering a reward for the capture of a notorious pirate. (visual–spatial)

CURRICULUM LINKS			
England	Literacy	Yr 1	• read non-fiction books and select information needed
Northern Ireland	English	KS 1	• read information books for writing tasks and collect information relevant to specific purposes
Republic of Ireland	English	1st/ 2nd	• engage with a wide variety of text and perform simple information retrieval tasks
Scotland	English	B	• use a wide selection of informational and reference texts
Wales	English	KS 1	• read information and make use of a range of sources of information

SHIPWRECKS

people wise

❶ Lighthouses are important to ships

because _____

_____

_____

_____

❷ Add to this list of dangers to ships.

strong winds _____

_____

_____

_____

❸ Record your information about a shipwreck.

Name of ship _____

It was sailing from _____

It was going to _____

The date was _____

It was wrecked because _____

_____

_____

The crew and passengers _____

The multiple intelligence focus for this activity is intrapersonal.

> An intrapersonal child understands and analyses his/her thoughts and feelings.
> He/She learns best through individual activities.

Objective

- Writes a self-description as a message in a bottle.

Preparation

- Prepare two bottles containing messages. One should look much older than the other.

Teacher information

- Stimulate children' interest in the older bottle you 'found' on the beach. Ask them to guess answers to who, when, where, what and why questions and to pose some questions of their own about the bottle and the message in the bottle.

  Sample message: *Hello, I'm so pleased that you found my message. I wonder who you are and when and where you found it. My name is Patrick, but my friends call me Paddy. This is the year 1941 and I am a soldier. I am feeling very sad and lonely because I miss my family and my dog, Buster. I am 20 years old and when I get home, I want to go to university and become a dentist. I hope I'll be leaving Cocos Island soon.*

- Discuss what they now know about Patrick.

- Show children the second bottle and ask them to tell the class what they would like to know about the writer of the message in the bottle. Then are to imagine themselves near a beach and to write their own messages.

Answers

Teacher check

Additional activities

- Discuss personal reactions to Patrick's message and ask each child to compose two questions to ask Patrick.

- Create a beach scene with message bottles on the sand and in the water. (visual–spatial)

CURRICULUM LINKS			
England	Literacy	Yr 2	• use story structure to write about own experience in same/similar form
Northern Ireland	English	KS 1	• express thoughts, feelings and imaginings
Republic of Ireland	English	1st/ 2nd	• write in a variety of genres
Scotland	English	B	• write imaginatively, given a model
Wales	English	KS 1	• write in response to a variety of stimuli, in a range of forms

MESSAGE IN A BOTTLE

Task — *You will write a message in a bottle, telling the person who finds it all about yourself.*

self wise

1 Write a message in this bottle. Tell the person who finds it all about yourself.

home? family?

when? pets?

hobbies?

why?

name?

age? feelings?

2 Cut out your bottle and display it in your classroom.

THE SEA – MY SELF-ASSESSMENT

After completing this unit, I was able to ...

word wise	complete a wordsearch and answer 'What am I?' questions.	☆ ☆ ☆ ☆ ☆
logic wise	find and draw sea creatures on a grid.	☆ ☆ ☆ ☆ ☆
nature wise	complete an information chart about endangered sea life.	☆ ☆ ☆ ☆ ☆
picture wise	create an underwater diorama.	☆ ☆ ☆ ☆ ☆
body wise	role-play animals and people at the beach and make up and perform short plays.	☆ ☆ ☆ ☆ ☆
music wise	sing and make up rounds about the sea.	☆ ☆ ☆ ☆ ☆
people wise	work in a small group to find out and write about a shipwreck.	☆ ☆ ☆ ☆ ☆
self wise	write a message about myself to put in bottle.	☆ ☆ ☆ ☆ ☆

What I learnt

TOYS

Informational text ---- ☐ ☐ ---- Plan a play

word wise · Teddy bear's picnic ---- ☐ ☐ ---- Musical toys · *music wise*

logic wise · Toys on TV ---- ☐ ☐ ---- Old toys, new toys · *people wise*

nature wise · Toy T-shirts ---- ☐ ☐ ---- My toy time line · *self wise*

picture wise · Baby toy advertisement ---- ☐ ☐ ---- My self-assessment

What I know	What I want to know

Keywords

Name:	Date:

TOYS OVERVIEW

Verbal–Linguistic

- Deliver a speech to the class or write a report about a favourite toy and why it is special.

- Pretend to be a toy and write your story, telling where and with whom you live, your likes and dislikes and what you hope will happen in your future.

- Discuss health and safety issues associated with toys, such as wearing helmets when riding a bike, using elbow or knee pads when rollerblading or skateboarding and playing in safe places.

- Debate the topics 'Toys are better than television' and 'Toys should be allowed at school'.

- Have the children write a letter to Santa about their Christmas toy wish list.

- Ask children to write stories about what they would do if their favourite toys came to life.

- Children write what they would say to their parents if they were asking for a new toy they really wanted. They should give reasons why they should have the toy, why they want it and what the benefits might be for the whole family.

Naturalist

- Make a list of toy animals.

- Use natural objects or materials to create a toy and describe how you could play with it.

- Visit an historical museum or a house to view and compare olden-day toys and games.

- Discuss what happens to old toys and games. Can they be recycled? What are the benefits?

- Use recycled materials to design a toy such as a robot.

- Design a soft toy based on a real animal, recreating its markings. Suitable animals might be zebras, leopards or killer whales.

Logical–Mathematical

- Measure and record the length and weight of different toys.

- Using a toy catalogue and a given budget, children decide which toys they would buy and how much change they would get.

- Decide how to sort a collection of toys by attributes such as size, colour, materials and what they do.

- Compare toys that float and sink and write about their features.

- Collect information about toys and games that were played with long ago and are still played with today. Examine the similarities and differences.

- Create tangram toys.

- Survey the class to find out their favourite toys and then create a graph using the information.

- Order toys according to their value.

Visual–Spatial

- Create a poster to advertise a toy fair.

- Design a special occasion outfit for a doll or teddy bear to wear.

- Children draw a toy they would like to have.

- Paint a toyshop mural of the class's favourite toys.

- Make a collage of toy photographs from catalogues and magazines.

- Design a wanted poster for a lost toy.

- Watch the film *Toy story* and then ask the children to design another toy they think could have been in the film. They could also add details about its character.

- Have older people visit the classroom with toys they had when they were the age of the children. The children could compare these toys to their favourite toys.

- Invent a new toy. Draw it and label its special features. How much would it cost? Where could people buy it?

TOYS OVERVIEW

Bodily–Kinaesthetic

- Role-play toy movements; e.g. toy soldiers, robots, cars, trucks, animals.
- Role-play shopping in a classroom toyshop using toy money.
- Construct Lego™ models of cars, trucks etc. Experiment to find out which ones travel furthest or fastest, hold the most, are biggest or smallest etc.
- Construct doll's house furniture made from everyday materials.
- Make paper dolls complete with changeable outfits.

Interpersonal

- Work in a small group to create a board game for children.
- Survey people in your class to find the most and least popular toys.
- Discuss the reasons for putting age limits on toys and the meaning of labels such as 'Not suitable for children under three years'.

Musical–Rhythmic

- Write a list of toys that make noises.
- Take turns to make or describe toy noises and have the class guess the mystery toys.
- Create a song for a 'talking' toy such as a doll.
- Move to words associated with toys; e.g. 'roll', 'spin', 'fast', 'slow', 'fly', 'bounce'. Perform these movements to the beat of percussion instruments or other rhythmic sounds.
- Listen to Tchaikovsky's *Nutcracker suite* and ask the children to describe what they think might be happening.
- Move as wind-up toys while appropriate music is playing.
- Write and perform a radio jingle to advertise a toy you have invented.

Intrapersonal

- Children write about the first toy they can remember.
- Ask the children to write five reasons why they think children like to play with toys.
- Complete a design brief for a toy that rocks.
- Children write about what effects toy advertisements in catalogues or on television have on them personally.
- Write a letter or an email to your favourite toy, telling it how much you like it, why you like it so much and what your favourite times spent with the toy were.
- Research to find out some facts about the history of one of your favourite toys.
- Ask the children to write their opinions on toys that are created because of films or television programmes.

TOYS
INFORMATIONAL TEXT

Do you like playing with toys? Children all over the world do—and even some adults!

Changing toys

The toys you like now will be very different from those you played with when you were younger. For example, a lot of baby toys are soft, make sounds and are easy for the baby to hold. Toys like these help to improve the sight and hearing of babies.

Some toys help children of different ages to learn things, like jigsaw puzzles or card games. Other toys help children to use their imaginations, like puppets or action figures. But no matter what your age, all toys have one thing in common – they are fun!

Toys of the past

Children have always enjoyed playing with toys. Many types of toys that were played with in the past are still enjoyed by children today. In ancient times, children liked to play with toys like hoops, dolls and marbles. These toys were made by hand. Sometimes they were played with in a different way from the way children would play with them now.

Hoops were once made from twisted reeds, vines, wood or metal. In 1957, the first plastic hoop was made.

Dolls were once made from wood, cloth and terracotta. Over the years, they have become more beautiful and lifelike. Most dolls that you see today have been made in factories. A wide variety of materials are used, like plastic, china and cloth. The Barbie Doll was the first doll to have an adult-shaped body. She was created in 1958.

Marbles were first made from stone or baked clay. Now machines make them from plastic and glass. Some of the games ancient children once played with marbles are still played today.

TOYS
INFORMATIONAL TEXT

Toys today

Some of the toys that children of today like playing with are board games, teddy bears, action figures and electronic games.

Children all over the world like to play board games. Some popular board games are Trivial Pursuit, Scrabble, Monopoly, chess and draughts. Some board games are electronic.

Many children today also play with action figures, such as robots that can 'transform' into other things. Other action figures are based on characters from films or television shows.

Most children today have played with hand-held computer games. The first ones were made in the 1970s and were very simple compared to those you can buy now! Today, the games are quicker and more colourful. You can even watch some in 3-D!

Many children have a teddy bear. But did you know that this toy got its name from an American president in the 1900s? The president's first name was Theodore, but people called him 'Teddy'. One day, a newspaper printed a cartoon that showed the president with a bear cub. Not long after, soft toys called 'teddy bears' were made.

Toys from other countries

Children from other countries may play with toys you have not heard of.

In Russia, children play with Matryoshka dolls. They are different-sized wooden dolls that fit inside each other.

In Indonesia, children play a board game called congklak. It is played on a board with holes and shells.

In India, children play a game with a top called a lattoo. A string is used to throw the lattoo to the ground. The player whose lattoo spins the longest is the winner.

The multiple intelligence focus for this activity is verbal–linguistic.

> A verbal–linguistic child thinks in words.
> He/She learns best through activities involving reading, writing and speaking.

Objective

- Plans and writes an invitation for a picnic.

Preparation

- Show examples of invitations to class prior to giving out the worksheet.

- Children will need extra paper or card to create their invitations.

Teacher information

- Before the children begin the worksheet, teachers should discuss the format of an invitation. Examples of different types of invitations should be shown and the common headings used written on the board; for example, 'Time', 'Date', 'Place', 'RSVP'.

- Teachers should read the information at the top of the page and read the places on the map to the children. A short discussion could be held about which places would be best for a picnic. The children could orally describe how to get to each place from the car park; e.g. 'To get to the rose garden, walk between the mini-golf and the tennis court. The rose garden is right in front of the mini-golf'.

- After the children have completed Question 1, the other questions can be read aloud and discussed, particularly Question 5. The children may suggest that the people they are inviting will need to know information about what to wear or what else they should bring to the picnic.

- Once the worksheet is completed, the children can create their invitations on separate sheets of paper or card. They could choose whether the invitation is folded over or is simply written on one side of the sheet. Teachers should remind them to use the headings that were written on the board. The children can then decorate their invitations. Some could be read aloud to the class.

Answers

Teacher check

Additional activities

- Write a creative narrative about what might happen at a teddy bear's picnic.

CURRICULUM LINKS			
England	English	KS 1	• write to communicate to others
Northern Ireland	English	KS 1	• write in a variety of forms, including invitations
Republic of Ireland	English	1st/ 2nd	• write in a variety of genres, e.g. invitations
Scotland	English	B	• use simple notes to order functional writing
Wales	English	KS 1	• write in a range of forms, e.g. invitations

TEDDY BEAR'S PICNIC

Task — *You will plan and write an invitation to a picnic.*

 You are helping to organise a toy festival. You decide to hold a teddy bear's picnic for families. It will be held in Pleasant Park on 1 September.

Pleasant Park

freshwater lake

tree

duck pond

rose garden

tree

mini-golf

car park

tree

tree

tree

woodland walk

playground

tree

tree

tree

tennis court

1. Decide on the best picnic spot. Describe how to get there from the car park.

_____

_____

2. What time of day do you think is best for the picnic? Say why.

_____

_____

3. List the games or other activities that will happen during the picnic.

4. If people don't have a teddy bear, what other toys can they bring instead?

_____

_____

_____

5. Write anything else people need to know about your picnic.

_____

_____

6. Use your plan to create an invitation to the picnic on a separate sheet of paper.

The multiple intelligence focus for this activity is logical–mathematical.

A logical–mathematical child thinks rationally and in abstractions.
He/She learns best through activities involving problem-solving, numbers and patterns.

Objectives

- Counts the number of different types of toy advertisements shown during a children's television show.
- Answers questions about the data contained in a table.

Preparation

- Teachers will need to record a children's television programme of at least one hour's duration. Toy advertisements are most likely to be screened during the 6.30 am – 8.30 am or 3.30 pm – 5.00 pm timeslots on weekdays or during any children's television programmes or films shown on the weekends. During a one-hour children's show, approximately 20 – 30 advertisements will be shown, with a varying number of these being for toys.
- The advertisements will need to be shown to the children at the beginning of the lesson. The television programme itself could be fast-forwarded.

Teacher information

- Explain to the children that they are going to watch the advertisements that were shown during a recent children's television programme. After the name of the programme has been written on the worksheet, the advertisements should then be shown. After each advertisement finishes, teachers should pause the vision. The children should then write a tally mark next to the heading 'Number of advertisements' and write what type of advertisement it was (once a heading has already been written, there is no need to write it again). If the advertisement shown is for a toy, the children should also write a tally mark in the appropriate space under 'Type of toys'. This activity should be done as a class so the data is the same for each child.
- When all the advertisements have been viewed, the children should complete Question 2 individually. The answer to Question 2 (d) could be discussed as a class.

Answers

Teacher check

Additional activities

- Survey the class to find out which are the most popular toy advertisements on television. Show the results as a graph. (logical–mathematical)
- Create television advertisements for toys in small groups (bodily–kinaesthetic).

CURRICULUM LINKS			
England	Numeracy	Yr 1/2	• solve problems by sorting, classifying and organising information in simple ways
Northern Ireland	Maths	KS 1	• collect, record and interpret data
Republic of Ireland	Maths	1st/ 2nd	• represent, read and interpret simple tables
Scotland	Maths	B	• collect and organise information using a tally sheet
Wales	Maths	KS 1	• collect, record and interpret data

TOYS ON TV

You will count the different types of advertisements shown during a children's TV show and find the most common type of toy advertised.

1 Watch the advertisements shown during a children's TV show to complete the table.

Name of show	
Number of advertisements	
Types of advertisements (e.g. toys, food, cars)	
Number of toy advertisements	

Types of toys
Number of advertisements

soft toys	
action figures	
dolls	
board games	
computer games	
other toys	

2 Answer the questions below.

(a) How many advertisements were for toys?

_____

(b) How many advertisements were for other things?

_____

(c) Which type of toys were the most advertisements for?

_____

(d) Why do you think this is?

_____

_____

The multiple intelligence focus for this activity is naturalist.

> A naturalist child has an awareness of the patterns in nature.
> He/She learns best through activities involving animals, plants and the environment.

Objectives

- Uses natural objects to create a T-shirt design.
- Explains his/her reasons for choosing the natural objects used for a design.

Preparation

- Each child will need a plain T-shirt in a bright colour.
- Teachers will need to supply a collection of natural objects such as leaves, petals, twigs, pebbles, shells, nuts, sand or feathers. These should be in boxes at the front of the classroom for children to collect. Alternatively, the children could collect their own natural objects to use for this activity and bring them to the classroom.
- Teachers will need a sample T-shirt that has already been sprayed with bleach to reveal a toy design.
- One or more spray bottles containing bleach and buckets of cold water will need to be set up outside. The T-shirts should be sprayed on a flat concrete surface away from objects that may be damaged by the bleach.
- Adult helpers will be required to spray and then rinse each child's T-shirt. Adult helpers should wear rubber gloves for this activity.
- Note: For safety reasons, the children should be kept away from the bleach. They should also not wear their T-shirts until they have been thoroughly washed in a washing machine.

Teacher information

- Introduce the activity by showing the children the sample T-shirt and explaining how the design was created. The natural objects they can use for their designs can be shown.
- Read Question 1 to the children and have them draw and label their toy design. Teachers should guide the children to draw simple designs.
- Discuss the designs and ask the children to suggest some of the natural objects that could be used for different features. They should consider the texture and shapes of the objects. Tell the children that when the bleach is sprayed on the shirt, only the outline of the objects will be seen.
- Have the children arrange their objects on the T-shirts and then give the T-shirts to adult helpers. The helpers should spray the bleach lightly around the edges of the objects. When the colour starts to change (allow approximately one minute) the objects should be disposed of.
- While the adult helpers are spraying and rinsing the shirt, the children should complete Question 4 individually, focusing on the features of the natural objects they chose.
- The children can then complete Question 5.

Answers

Teacher check

Additional activities

- Make and decorate a simple toy such as a sock puppet or a jack-in-the-box using natural or recycled objects.

CURRICULUM LINKS			
England	Art & design	KS 1	• use a range of materials and processes
Northern Ireland	Art & design	KS 1	• use a range of materials and processes
Republic of Ireland	Visual arts	1st/ 2nd	• discover the possibilities of fabric as media for imaginative expression
Scotland	Art & design	A	• use given materials to solve a simple task
Wales	Art	KS 1	• make images using a range of materials and processes

TOY T-SHIRTS

1 Choose a toy you would like to see on a T-shirt. It might be a teddy bear, a jack-in-the-box, a kite, a wind-up car—or something else. Draw and label a picture of it.

2 Collect the natural objects you want to use for your design. For example, shells could make wheels, a leaf could make a mouth or some feathers could make hair.

3 Place the objects on your T-shirt. When you are happy with your design, ask an adult to spray it with bleach and then rinse the T-shirt in cold water.

4 Draw the objects you used and complete the table.

Object	What it made	Why I chose it

5 Check your T-shirt. Write what you like best about it.

_____

_____

The multiple intelligence focus for this activity is visual–spatial.

A visual–spatial child thinks in images, colours and shape.
He/She learns best through activities involving visualisation.

Objective

- Creates an advertisement for a baby toy.

Preparation

- The children will require drawing materials such as crayons or coloured pencils.

- Teachers may like to collect some examples of appropriate soft baby toys and some toy catalogues to show the children.

Teacher information

- Before the worksheet is given to the children, teachers may like to show some baby toys. Discuss the colours, sounds and materials that have been used and why they may have been used. For example, many baby toys are made of soft material or plastic. They do not have sharp parts or hard edges to hurt the baby when he/she sucks on the toy to explore it. There must be no loose parts to chew off or break off and be swallowed. The materials must also be non-toxic.

- Before the children complete Question 2, show them some toy catalogue advertisements. Discuss the colours that have been used. The children can then complete Question 2.

Answers

Teacher check

Additional activities

- View a range of toys designed for different age groups and list their features. (visual–spatial)

- Survey different-aged children in the school about their favourite toys. (interpersonal).

CURRICULUM LINKS			
England	Art & design	KS 1	• answer questions about the starting points for their work, develop ideas and design and make images
Northern Ireland	Art & design	KS 1	• use resource and reference materials to develop ideas
Republic of Ireland	Science	1st/ 2nd	• communicate a plan of action using appropriate vocabulary
Scotland	Art & design	A	• produce images expressing personal ideas
Wales	Art	KS 1	• make images for a variety of purposes, using a range of materials

BABY TOY ADVERTISEMENT

Task *You will design and label a picture for an advertisement for a baby toy that makes sounds.*

picture wise

1 Plan your drawing using the headings below.

Tick or write the type of toy you want in the advertisement.

☐ animal toy   ☐ doll   ☐ ball

☐ rattle   ☐ squeaky toy   ☐ other _____

Make up a name for the toy.	What kinds of materials will it be made from?
What sounds will it make?	
What colours are on the toy?	Draw a plan of your picture.
List other special features.	
How much will it cost?	

2 Use your ideas to draw your picture for the advertisement on a separate sheet of paper. Label its special features and write the price of the toy.

The multiple intelligence focus for this activity is bodily–kinaesthetic.

> A bodily–kinaesthetic child has good physical awareness.
> He/She learns best through 'hands-on' activities.

Objective

- Uses his/her face, voice and body to show feelings during an improvisation.

Preparation

- The children will need to be organised into groups of three.

Teacher information

- Read the information at the top of the worksheet to the children. Discuss some possible scenarios for why the toys have gone missing; for example, a younger child has taken them outside for a tea party; the toys have come to life and are completing the children' work for them in a corner of the classroom. The children can then complete Question 1 in their groups.

- Read each of the statements in Question 2 to the class. Ways of showing different feelings should be discussed; e.g. 'I could show I am worried by wrinkling my forehead, speaking quickly and wringing my hands'. The children should then complete the statements individually, based on their group decisions for Question 1.

- Allow the groups about 15 – 20 minutes to practise their improvisations. They can then be performed for the class.

Answers

- Teacher check

Additional activities

- Have the children demonstrate what they would do in other situations involving toys; e.g. if a toy came to life.

- Write the script of the plays you created. (verbal–linguistic)

CURRICULUM LINKS			
England	English	KS 1	• create and sustain roles individually and when working with others
Northern Ireland	English	KS 1	• take part in drama activities, including role-play
Republic of Ireland	Drama	1st/ 2nd	• re-enact for others a scene that has been made in small-group work
Scotland	Drama	B	• sustain and develop a role and participate in small-scale presentations
Wales	English	KS 1	• participate in drama activities, improvisation and performances of varying kinds

PLAN A PLAY

In a group of three, plan a play about some missing toys. Here is the story you will need to show.

You have each brought a favourite toy to school for news. But when you come back from lunch, your toys are missing. You search for them and finally find them—somewhere surprising!

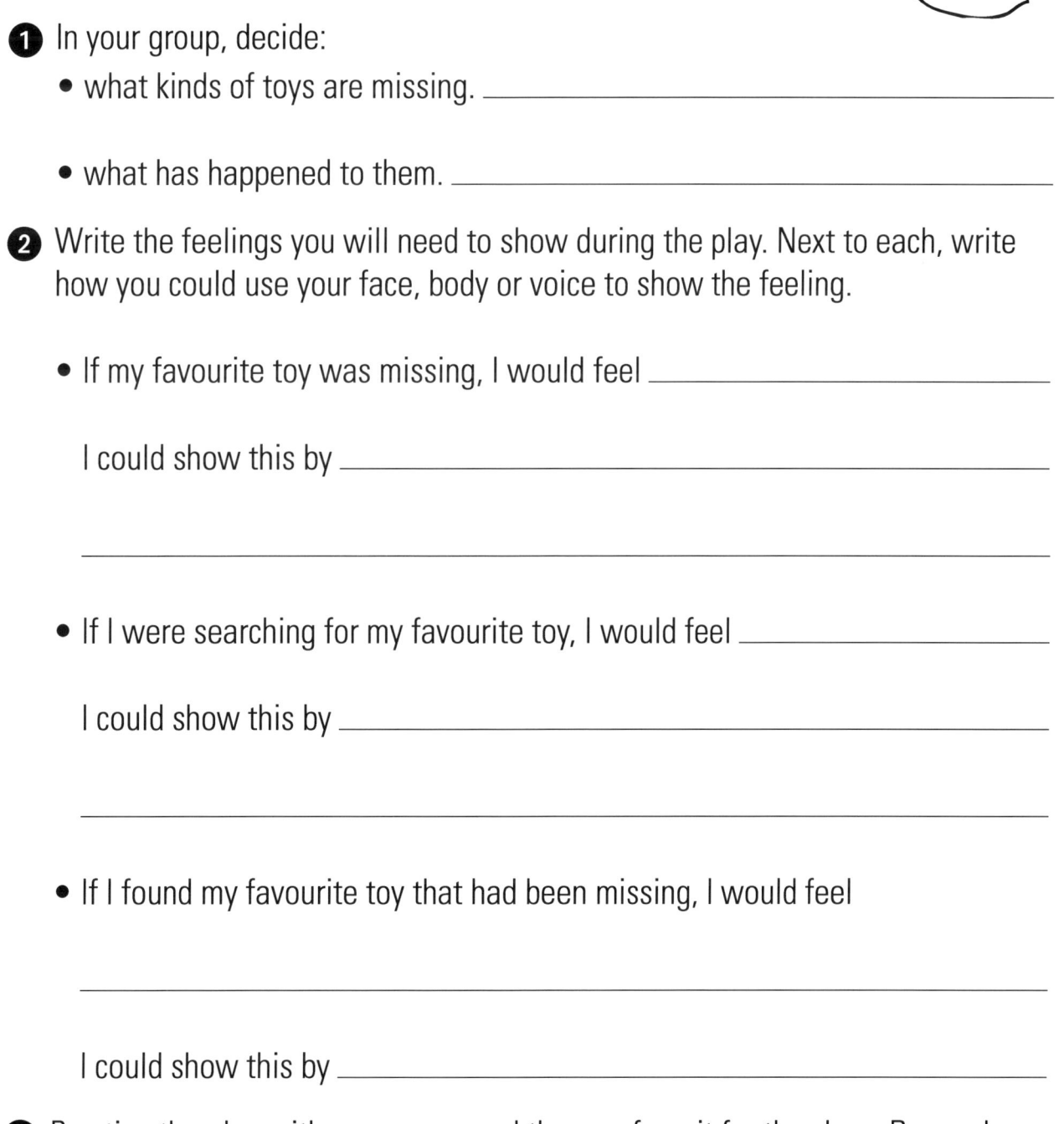

1. In your group, decide:
   - what kinds of toys are missing. _____

   - what has happened to them. _____

2. Write the feelings you will need to show during the play. Next to each, write how you could use your face, body or voice to show the feeling.

   - If my favourite toy was missing, I would feel _____

     I could show this by _____

     _____

   - If I were searching for my favourite toy, I would feel _____

     I could show this by _____

     _____

   - If I found my favourite toy that had been missing, I would feel

     _____

     I could show this by _____

3. Practise the play with your group and then perform it for the class. Remember to show the feelings you wrote about.

The multiple intelligence focus for this activity is musical–rhythmic.

> A musical–rhythmic child has an awareness of music and sound.
> He/She learns best through activities involving music or rhythms.

Objectives

- Records his/her thoughts and feelings about a piece of music.
- Moves as a toy to a piece of music.

Preparation

- Teachers will need to find a suitable piece of music for this activity. It is suggested that instrumental music is used. Some suggested music includes pieces from Saint-Saens' *Carnival of the animals*, Jeff Wayne's *War of the worlds* and pieces from Prokofiev's *Peter and the wolf*. Excerpts from music written for classical ballets (e.g. *Swan Lake*, *Coppelia*) would also be suitable. This activity could be repeated a number of times, using varying pieces of music on each occasion.
- A large open area suitable for the children to move to the music will be required.

Teacher information

- Ask the children to close their eyes and then play the prepared music piece for them. Teachers may like to ask the children to orally describe what the music was like before they complete Question 1.
- Teachers should then play the music again, asking the children to imagine what sort of toy might be moving to the music. The children can then complete Questions 3 – 6. Teachers may like to play the music softly while the children are writing and drawing.
- After sharing some of the answers to Questions 3 to 6, teachers should play the music again, while all the children move to it. Encourage the children to concentrate on their own movements.

Answers

None required

Additional activities

- Make up small group 'toy' dances to different pieces of music.
- Watch excerpts from classical ballets on television that involve toys; e.g. Tchaikovsky's *Nutcracker suite* and Delibes' *Coppelia*. Discuss how the dancers move to the music.

CURRICULUM LINKS			
England	Music	KS 1	• explore and express ideas and feelings about music using movement
Northern Ireland	Music	KS 1	• respond imaginatively to short pieces of music
Republic of Ireland	Music	1st/2nd	• respond imaginatively to pieces of music through movement and illustrate responses in a variety of ways
Scotland	Music	B	• listen to short extracts of music and become aware of effects and moods created
Wales	Music	KS 1	• respond to music through movement and/or other forms of expression

MUSICAL TOYS

Task — You will describe what a piece of music makes you think of and move like a toy to a piece of music.

music wise

1 Listen to a piece of music with your eyes closed. Write some words to describe the music and how it made you feel.

2 Listen to the music again. Imagine what sort of toy might be moving to it.

3 What sort of toy did you imagine? _____

4 How was the toy moving? _____

5 Why was the toy moving like this?

6 Draw a picture of the toy you imagined.

7 Pretend you are the toy and move to the music as it plays again.

The multiple intelligence focus for this activity is interpersonal.

An interpersonal child enjoys being in groups or teams.
He/She learns best through activities involving working with others.

Objectives

- Interviews an older person about the past.
- Discusses ideas in a group.

Preparation

- The children will need to work in groups of three.
- Each group will need scrap paper and pens to write all the toys talked about by the interviewees.
- Arrange a number of grandparents or other older people to be interviewed about the toys they used to play with as children of approximately the same age as the children. The interviewees should be stationed around the room to be interviewed by the groups. Each group should talk to at least two older people.

Teacher information

- Each group of children talks to at least two older people about the toys they played with when they were the age of the children. One member of each group could write the answers given on a sheet of paper. The group can then write five of these answers for Question 1 on the worksheet. The groups should then complete Question 2. Encourage the groups to take ideas from each member of their group when composing their lists.
- After the groups have completed Question 3, teachers could ask some of the children to share their answers before the groups complete Question 4.

Answers

- Teacher check

Additional activities

- Ask small groups of children to discuss whether they think toys are 'better' today. (verbal–linguistic)
- Research to find out about some toys of the past. (intrapersonal)

CURRICULUM LINKS			
England	English	KS 1	• speak to different people, including other adults
Northern Ireland	English	KS 1	• take turns at talking and listening
Republic of Ireland	English	1st/ 2nd	• engage in real situations involving language use
Scotland	English	C	• select questions appropriate to the purpose of an interview and interview visitors to the school
Wales	English	KS 1	• talk to different audiences, including other adults

OLD TOYS, NEW TOYS

people wise

1 In a group of three, talk to some older people to find out what their favourite toys were when they were your age. List five of these toys.

1	
2	
3	
4	
5	

2 With your group, make a list of five toys that are popular with children your age now.

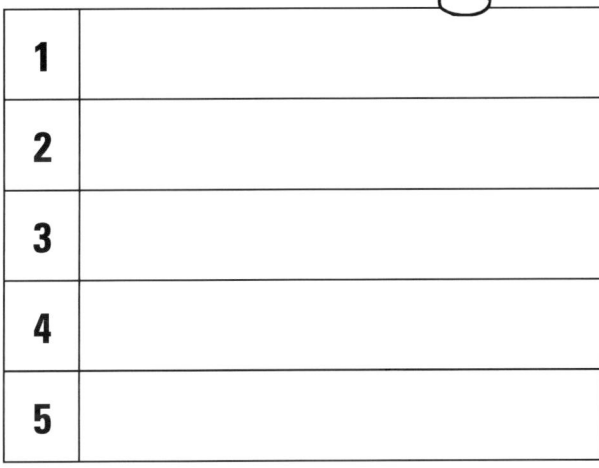

1	
2	
3	
4	
5	

3 In your group, compare the two lists.

(a) Were there any toys you wrote for both lists?   **yes**   **no**

Why do you think this might be? _____

_____

(b) Do any of you play with any of the toys on the 'older' list?   **yes**   **no**

Why/Why not? _____

_____

4 Write a list of five toys your group thinks children your age might be playing with in 50 years' time. Share your list with the class.

1	
2	
3	
4	
5	

The multiple intelligence focus for this activity is intrapersonal.

An intrapersonal child understands and analyses his/her thoughts and feelings.
He/She learns best through individual activities.

Objective

- Creates a time line of toys he/she has played with.

Preparation

- Teachers should ask the children to talk to their parents to find out what their favourite toys were when they were younger.

Teacher information

- The children should complete Questions 1 and 2 individually. The answers could then be discussed with the class.

Answers

- Teacher check

Additional activities

- Make a list of the types of toys the children enjoyed playing with in the past. Create a graph to show which were the most popular. (logical–mathematical)

CURRICULUM LINKS			
England	History	KS 1	• recognise changes in their own lives and place events/objects in chronological order
Northern Ireland	History	KS 1	• place objects in sequence and build up time lines of their life now and in the past
Republic of Ireland	History	1st/ 2nd	• construct simple, personal time line
Scotland	Society	A	• sequence events in their lives and talk about objects from their past
Wales	History	KS 1	• sequence events and objects

MY TOY TIME LINE

You will create a time line of the toys you played with at different ages.

self wise

1 Draw and write about three toys you have played with at different ages to make a time line.

Describe this toy. _____

_____

I think a baby would like this toy because …

_____

_____

Describe this toy. _____

_____

I think a toddler would like this toy because …

_____

_____

Describe this toy. _____

_____

I like this toy because …

_____

_____

2 What sort of toys do you think you might be playing with two years from now?

_____

TOYS – MY SELF-ASSESSMENT

After completing this unit, I was able to ...

word wise	plan and write an invitation to a picnic.	☆ ☆ ☆ ☆ ☆
logic wise	count the different types of toy advertisements during a children's TV show and find the most common type of toy advertised.	☆ ☆ ☆ ☆ ☆
nature wise	use natural objects to create a T-shirt design and explain why the objects were chosen.	☆ ☆ ☆ ☆ ☆
picture wise	design and label an advertisement for a baby toy that makes sounds.	☆ ☆ ☆ ☆ ☆
body wise	use my face, body and voice to show feelings during a play.	☆ ☆ ☆ ☆ ☆
music wise	describe what a piece of music makes me think of and move like a toy to a piece of music.	☆ ☆ ☆ ☆ ☆
people wise	interview people about the past and discuss ideas in a group.	☆ ☆ ☆ ☆ ☆
self wise	create a time line of toys played with at different ages.	☆ ☆ ☆ ☆ ☆

What I learnt

Community

Informational text .... ☐ ☐ .... Pottery places

word wise

The community that people built .... ☐ ☐ .... Rhythmic names

music wise

logic wise

House survey .... ☐ ☐ .... 3-D community

people wise

nature wise

Special places .... ☐ ☐ .... Community problems

self wise

picture wise

Community map .... ☐ ☐ .... My self-assessment

What I know	What I want to know

Keywords

Name: _____ Date: _____

COMMUNITY OVERVIEW

Verbal–Linguistic

- Interview parents or adults about their responsibilities or roles in the community.
- List the responsibilities of people who work in the school community.
- Write a report on different occupations that help our community; e.g. shopkeeper, doctor, firefighter.
- Write a diary on 'A day in the life of a ...' (doctor, nurse etc.).
- Conduct an interview with a person from the local community.
- Plan and hold a morning tea for senior citizens in the community or invite them for special events such as the Harvest festival.
- Write a letter to someone who doesn't live in your community telling them all the great things about your community.
- Label a map of your community, showing all the places you like to go.
- Write 'What am I?' clues for community occupations.
- Collect articles from the local community newspaper to write a brief summary (or caption) about and collate into a booklet.
- Communicate by email with a class from a different community.

Logical–Mathematical

- Sort the services or amenities found in your community into appropriate categories; e.g. 'recreation – parks, basketball court, sports centre'.
- Conduct a survey about the occupations of parents. Collate and discuss.
- Make a map of the local community from a bird's-eye view, including shops, homes, schools, parks and other places of importance.
- Classify, compare and contrast the different occupations in the community or in different types of communities.
- Compile flow charts of community helpers' jobs.
- Categorise pictures of occupations and equipment used.
- Compare and contrast various communities; e.g. busy city, town, village, farming community.
- Give directions on a map to tell how to get from home to the video/DVD shop or to school.
- Record local weather statistics.

Naturalist

- Label pictures of some of the native plants found in the local community.
- Go on a 'nature walk' in the community to collect natural materials and use them to make a collage.
- Go on a field trip to explore features of the local community.
- Research and display information about people who work in the community to save the environment.
- Observe and record the animals that are in the local community. Investigate ways to keep them safe.
- Research a product from its source to the shop; e.g. milk, cereal.
- Identify any special natural features in the community. Discuss ways to preserve them.
- Plan a tourist walk or excursion for the local community.
- Plant trees in the local community.
- Collect and press local flowers.
- Compile a list of lakes, rivers, dams or beaches in the local area.
- Compile a list of ways local waterways could be conserved.

Visual–Spatial

- Create simple maps showing the different businesses found at a local shopping centre.
- Create a logo that represents your local community.
- Build a model of your community.
- Construct a skyscraper city using milk cartons of different sizes.
- Design a diorama to suit something of importance in the community.
- Design and make a poster which highlights something special in your community.
- Make a textured mural which shows different aspects of the local community.
- Invite a local or community artist into the school or classroom for children to observe him/her painting.
- Draw a portrait of yourself at a favourite local facility.
- Use material scraps to make collage pictures of people in the community.
- Make models of people in the community.
- Draw signs found in the community. Write short sentences to explain what they mean.
- View a map of the local area and locate the school and children's streets.

MULTIPLE INTELLIGENCES

COMMUNITY OVERVIEW

Bodily–Kinaesthetic

- Mime some different occupations people in the local community might have for the class to guess.
- Take part in and train for a local or school fun run, walkathon or jogathon.
- Follow procedures for cooking foods to take to a senior citizens home.
- Take part in a community clean up.
- Dramatise a confrontation between someone damaging the local community and a concerned community member.
- Make pottery houses.
- Learn and practise emergency procedures for keeping people in the community safe, such as using emergency phone numbers, what to do in case of fire etc.
- Visit a local attraction in the community.

Musical–Rhythmic

- Invite a community band or orchestra to play for the class.
- Listen to different singing voices and styles. Investigate various community venues where singers and other artists may perform.
- Write a rap or a jingle describing a job in the community.
- Create a musical/dance routine or song with movements to perform for the residents of an aged care home.
- Conduct singalongs at assembly, similar to karaoke.
- Sing songs about people who work in the community; e.g. farmer, baker, doctor.
- Learn and perform songs known by the older generation, such as 'When you're smiling'.
- Learn and perform poems or action rhymes such as 'Here are grandma's glasses'.

Interpersonal

- Ask small groups of children to create a mural which shows some of the different people in the community.
- Visit local community centres such as a library, shopping centre or fire station and write about their importance to the community.
- In a group, discuss and list the good and bad features of your community. Devise ways to improve those features which need improving.
- With a partner, design a playground for the local community.
- In pairs, investigate one community occupation. Include details such as training, clothing, equipment, tasks etc.
- Visit an aged care facility to sing songs, make morning tea, to play games or to share stories or drawings.
- In groups, discuss things children like best about their community and things that could be added to make it better.
- Compare child's own community with a different one; e.g. city to country, or one from the past. Each member of the group may choose one aspect of the community to investigate.
- In small groups, compile a list of rules for the community; e.g. at the local swimming pool or playground.
- In groups, research different sporting facilities in the community.

Intrapersonal

- Ask children to choose a problem (such as litter) in the school community. Each child can write a list of actions the community could take to help solve the problem.
- Research a job in the community you would like to do. Write about why you would like to do this job and the types of things you would do.
- Research occupations in communities of the past; e.g. blacksmith or chimney sweep, and compare these to present day occupations. Discuss how and why occupations have changed.
- Prepare a questionnaire to interview an older person about his/her life – both past and present.
- Compile a list of local tourist attractions.

COMMUNITY
INFORMATIONAL TEXT

A community is a group of people who live in the same place.

Types of communities

There are many different types of communities. Some may be big and some may be small. Some communities may be rich and some may be poor. Some may be in the city or in the country, near mountains or beach. Some communities may be made up of farms, tents or tall buildings. Some communities may be in hot places and some may be in cold places.

Features of a community

Communities have places and features which people want to use and which are important to them. These include roads, buildings such as libraries and museums, sporting venues, memorials, monuments, hospitals, shops, train and bus stations, parks, schools and places to spend their leisure time, such as rivers, lakes, cinemas and theatres.

Homes in a community

A community may have different types of homes. This depends on what type of homes people want, how many people live in them and what they want to use them for. Homes may be built differently depending on the environment in which they are built. For example, a house in a hot climate may need verandas and other ways to keep the people in the house cool. A house in a cold climate may need things which heat the house.

The people in a community may have a big or small home. They may live in a flat, a bungalow, a caravan, a tent, a cottage or a mansion. The homes may be made from different materials and have different gardens.

COMMUNITY
INFORMATIONAL TEXT

Working in a community

People may live and work in their community or travel to another to work. They may have different occupations. Some people in the community have occupations which help other people. These include doctors, nurses, dentists, firefighters, police officers, postal workers, ambulance officers, lifesavers, chemists and school crossing attendants.

Others provide services or goods which people need. These include taxi drivers, bus drivers, rubbish collectors, newsagents, banks, takeaway food outlets, veterinarians, builders, plumbers, electricians, bricklayers, shop assistants, farmers, road workers and cleaners.

Rules and responsibilities in a community

Communities usually have rules or laws to follow.

There are people in the community whose job it is to make sure that rules are enforced and offenders punished if they disobey those rules. This makes sure that people are safe in a community. Police officers, council workers, security officers and environmental workers try to keep the people and places in the community safe. Families and schools have rules to protect children and to help them cooperate with each other.

They also give children and adults responsibilities so that the family and school runs smoothly and to make sure that everyone is treated fairly.

Looking after the community

People have a responsibility to look after the places in the community and to obey the rules. Places such as parks, rivers and lakes and community buildings need to be kept free from litter and graffiti. Plants, animals and trees need to be looked after so that species native to a particular environment are preserved.

The multiple intelligence focus for this task is verbal–linguistic.

> A verbal–linguistic child thinks in words.
> He/She learns best through activities involving reading, writing and speaking.

Objective

- Uses a familiar format to write information about a community.

Preparation

- Children should have read or been read the story *This is the house that Jack built* before commencing this activity.

- Children should have read the informational text on pages 92 and 93 before commencing this task.

Teacher information

- Discuss the story *This is the house that Jack built* and write the things and animals in the order they appear in the book.

- Show the relationship between each animal/person and the next.

- Write the community story below on the board and read it to the children. Underline the words indicated.

  'This is the *community* that people built.

  This is the *road* that runs through the community that people built.

  This is the *car,* that goes on the road, that runs through the community that people built.

  This is the *family,* that drives in the car, that goes on the road, that runs through the community that people built.

  This is the *child* that belongs in the family, that drives in the car, that goes on the road, that runs through the community that people built.'

- Write another on the board using child assistance using the word 'cinema' or 'sports ground'. It may be easier to start with place names than people to start with. Underline the important words. (See previous example.)

- Children read, write and select a community word to use in their story.

- Child attempt to write a story of their own.

Answers

- Teacher check

Additional activities

- Children complete a cloze activity using information about the community.

- Children complete a wordsearch using community words.

- Children write an acrostic using the word 'community'.

CURRICULUM LINKS			
England	Literacy	Yr 1	• use patterned stories as models for their own writing
Northern Ireland	English	KS 1	• write based upon experience of stories read or heard
Republic of Ireland	English	1st/ 2nd	• experience how story structure is organised by reading and listening to fiction and writing a version of a story told by the teacher
Scotland	English	B	• write imaginatively, based upon a model
Wales	English	KS 1	• write in response to a variety of stimuli

THE COMMUNITY THAT PEOPLE BUILT

Task *You will use a familiar format to write information about a community.*

word wise

1. Read the community words below and write some of your own.

library	fire station	park	bus	school	hospital	post office

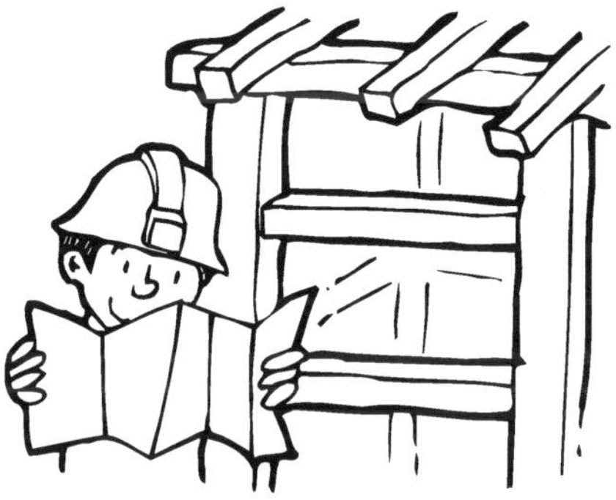

2. Choose one word from the list. ____________________

In the example read to you, the important words were: community, road, car, family, child.

3. Write important words which could follow your chosen word. ____________________

____

4. Write your community story using your chosen word and the words which follow from it. Finish each line with the words 'the community that people built.'

____

____

____

____

____

____

____

____

The multiple intelligence focus for this task is logical–mathematical.

A logical–mathematical child thinks rationally and in abstractions.
He/She learns best through activities involving problem-solving, numbers and patterns.

Objective

• Conducts a survey to gather information about homes in the local community.

Preparation

• Children view the homes visible from the school playground and discuss them in relation to the materials used, the size, the garden, the garage or carport etc.

• View posters or pictures of houses being built. If the children are lucky enough to live in a new housing estate where houses are being built, they may participate in a walking excursion to watch the progress of homes in the area.

Teacher information

• Children should be aware that houses look different and vary greatly inside.

• Read the instructions for conducting the survey with the children to ensure that they know what to do.

• Allow children to move around the room to complete the task.

• Children will need some time to look at their results before answering Questions 2 and 3.

• Children may wish to view magazine pictures and plans of houses before completing Question 4. They may also like to discuss their choice with a partner or small group.

• Children may create a 'fantasy' house as their ideal home. Allow children to be as creative as they wish. Discuss the advantages and disadvantages of some of the homes when they are completed.

Answers

Teacher check

Additional activities

• Children devise and complete a similar format to gather information about their own home. Compare this survey to that of another child.

• Children draw a detailed picture of their own home and add materials to create texture. Display in a community mural. Add streets, traffic, parks, schools and people. (visual–spatial)

CURRICULUM LINKS			
England	Geography	KS 1	• observe and record, e.g. identify buildings in the street
Northern Ireland	Geography	KS 1	• learn about the main features of their home
Republic of Ireland	Geography	1st/ 2nd	• recognise that people live in a variety of homes and develop an awareness and appreciation of different types of homes in the locality
Scotland	Society	B	• select and record information for a given purpose
Wales	Geography	KS 1	• collect and record information

HOUSE SURVEY

You will conduct a survey and collate information about homes in the local community.

Many homes in a community are different. Conduct a survey in your class to find out the different types of homes and how many there are of each.

1 Complete the boxes using information from eight class members.
Tick each box or write keywords.

Materials used	One/two storey	Number of rooms	Big/small garden	Type of shelter for the car(s)	Extras (pond, conservatory etc.)

2 From your survey, describe the most common type of home. _____

_____

3 Describe the least common type of home. _____

_____

4 On a separate sheet of paper, draw your ideal home.

The multiple intelligence focus for this task is naturalist.

> A naturalist child has an awareness of the patterns in nature.
> He/She learns best through activities involving animals, plants and the environment.

Objective

- Identifies special places in the community and gives reasons why they are special.

Preparation

- As a class, identify special features in the playground. This may include places such as the fixed equipment, an area of the garden, a favourite seat under the trees, the sandpit or the seats outside the classroom. Discuss reasons why they are special.

- Children identify places in their home or places they have visited which they consider special.

Teacher information

- List well-known places in the local community. Discuss the reason for them being special. Places such as memorials and places named after well-known local celebrities may be included.

- Discuss the things that may be found in these places to ensure that children include important details in their drawings.

- Children may complete the remainder of Question 1 independently but may wish to discuss answers to Question 2 with a partner.

Answers

- Teacher check

Additional activities

- Children describe how their special places make them feel. (intrapersonal)

- Children create an illustration or a 3-D model of their ideal special place. (bodily–kinaesthetic) Children write about it. (verbal–linguistic)

CURRICULUM LINKS			
England	Geography	KS 1	• express views of places and recognise how the environment can be sustained
Northern Ireland	English	KS 1	• write for a variety of purposes, including to express their thoughts
Republic of Ireland	Geography	1st/ 2nd	• identify and appreciate the natural and human features of the local environment and realise there is both an individual and community responsibility for taking care of the environment
Scotland	Society	C	• explain how the environment can be protected
Wales	Geography	KS 1	• communicate ideas, information and opinions

SPECIAL PLACES

1 Draw and label pictures of two places in your local community which are special and say why they are special.

_____   _____

_____   _____

_____   _____

_____   _____

2 List some ways to look after these special places.

_____

_____

_____

_____

_____

The multiple intelligence focus for this task is visual–spatial.

> A visual–spatial child thinks in images, colours and shape.
> He/She learns best through activities involving visualisation.

Objective

- Uses a map of a community to find specific places.

Preparation

- Children should view a variety of maps to understand the types of information provided.
- Children should understand what a bird's-eye view is to understand that maps are presented as though viewed from above.

Teacher information

- Discuss the places on the map and read any words which may be unfamiliar.
- Children answer the questions on the worksheet independently.
- Children may share their answers to Questions 1(c), (d) and (e).

Answers

1. (a) fire station, church, library, hospital, school, park, council building

   (b) – (e) Teacher check

Additional activities

- Children draw and label a map of the classroom.
- Children draw and label a map of their bedroom.
- Follow a local road map during a drive with their family.

CURRICULUM LINKS			
England	Geography	KS 1	• use maps and plans
Northern Ireland	Geography	KS 1	• use simple picture maps
Republic of Ireland	Geography	1st/ 2nd	• develop some awareness of maps
Scotland	Society	A	• identify main features on a simple map
Wales	Geography	KS 1	• use maps and plans

COMMUNITY MAP

1 Look at the map below and answer the questions.

Community map

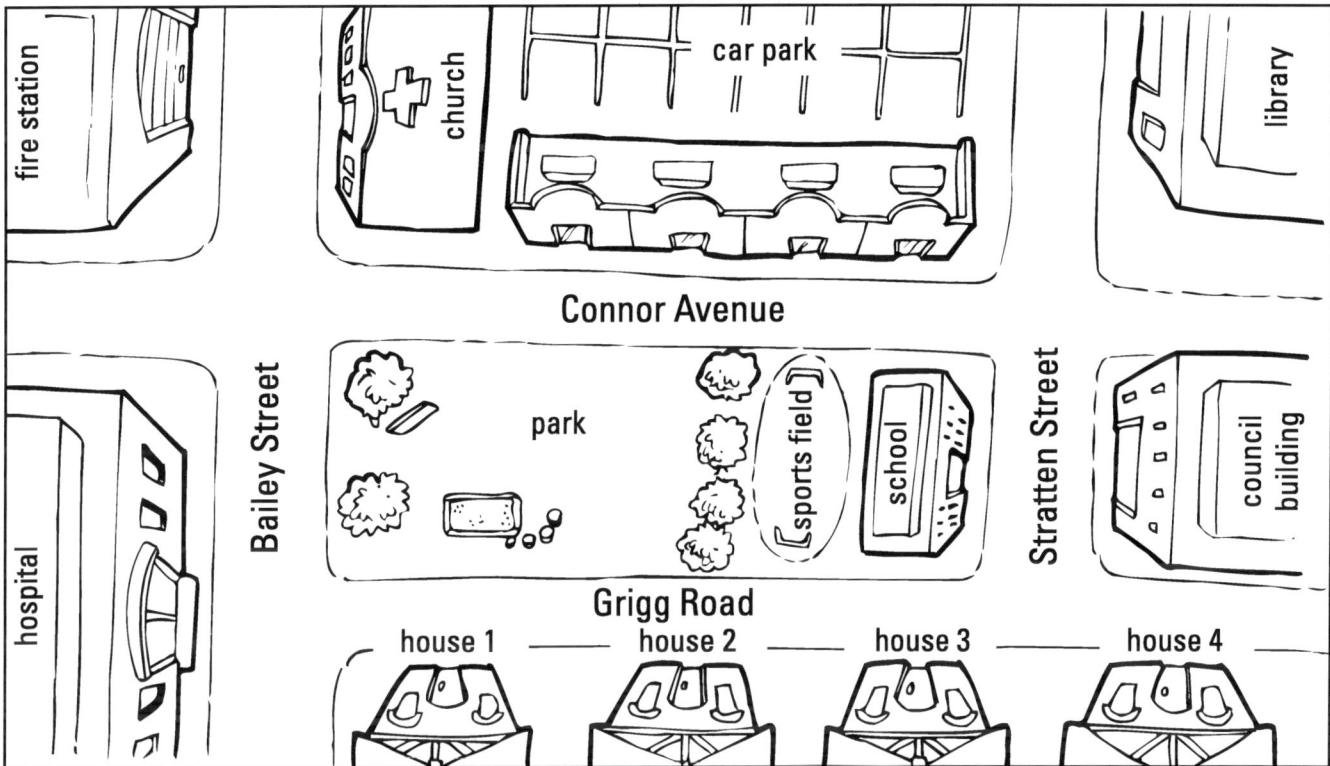

(a) Write the names of some important buildings on the map and then colour them.

_____

(b) Draw a path from house 4 to show the shortest way to get to the fire station.

(c) Write about the position of the car park. _____

_____

(d) Write which house would you like to live in and say why. _____

_____

_____

(e) Which street do you think is the most important? _____

Why? _____

The multiple intelligence focus for this task is bodily–kinaesthetic.

A bodily–kinaesthetic child has good physical awareness.
He/She learns best through 'hands-on' activities.

Objective

- Creates a pottery house.

Preparation

- Children should have practised making models from playdough and plasticine before completing this activity.

- Children will each need a ball of clay, two flat pieces of wood about 20 cm long and 1 cm thick, a placemat or clear plastic to work on, a variety of utensils to draw lines and shapes (matchsticks, toothpicks, old pencils etc.), a rolling pin, a blunt knife, a ball of playdough or plasticine for experimenting with textures and an old shirt or art shirt to protect themselves.

- Teachers may need a container of water to moisten balls of clay as they dry.

Teacher information

- Discuss the various basic shapes found in homes

- Discuss ways to create textures to represent tiles, planks of wood, bricks etc. At this time, allow children to experiment with ways to produce special effects. (The ball of playdough may be used for this.)

- Children may need to follow the procedure using a ball of plasticine or playdough first to make sure that they understand the instructions.

- Children should keep their house shape simple to begin with until they become more proficient potters.

- Excess clay may be used to add features as long as it is joined with a small amount of water or flattened securely to the main shape.

- Ensure that when children make the hole at the top (to allow for hanging), it is not too close to the edge. It must also be in the centre of the house, otherwise the house may not hang straight. Wide houses may require two evenly spaced holes at the top.

- If available, use a kiln to bake the houses then glaze them with various colours and bake again.

- Hang completed pottery houses from a piece of string suspended around the room or attach to a wall.

Answers

- Teacher check

Additional activities

- Make 3-D models of community buildings using recycled materials.

- Visit important community places such as the hospital, fire station, police station and ambulance station.

- View other pottery objects and discuss. (visual–spatial)

CURRICULUM LINKS			
England	Art & design	KS 1	• use a range of materials and processes
Northern Ireland	Art & design	KS 1	• explore the qualities of malleable materials
Republic of Ireland	Visual arts	1st/ 2nd	• experiment with and develop line, shape, texture and pattern in clay
Scotland	Art & design	B	• explore clay and how it is cut, shaped, joined and decorated
Wales	Art	KS 1	• make objects using a range of materials, tools, processes and techniques

POTTERY PLACES

Task · *You will create a pottery house.*

Use the procedure below to create a pottery house.

1

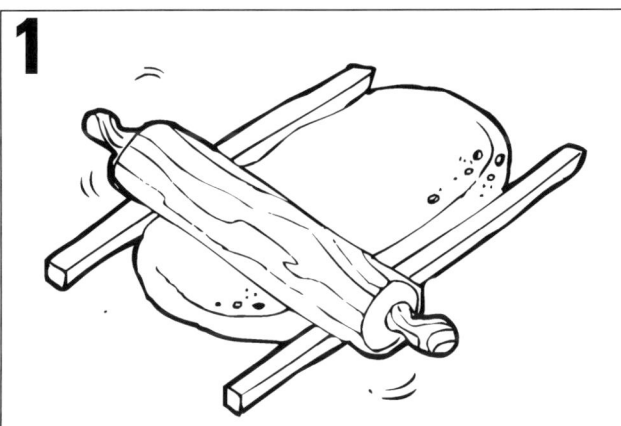

Roll the clay between the wood until it is an even thickness.

2

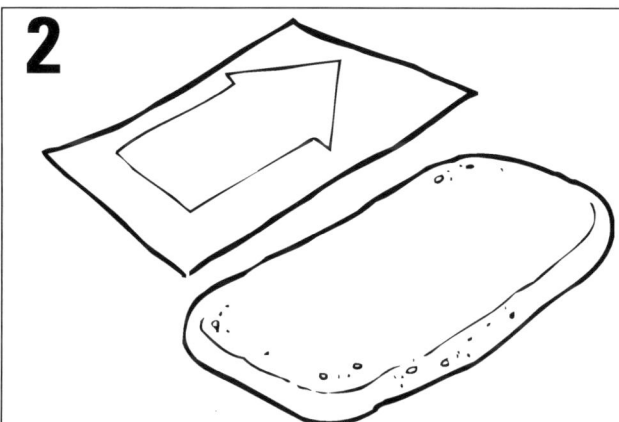

Use paper about the same size as the clay to draw a simple house shape.

3

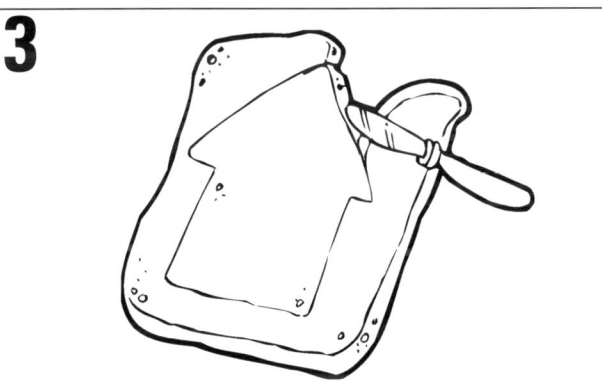

Cut out the house, place it on the clay and trace around it with the knife. Remove the extra clay.

4

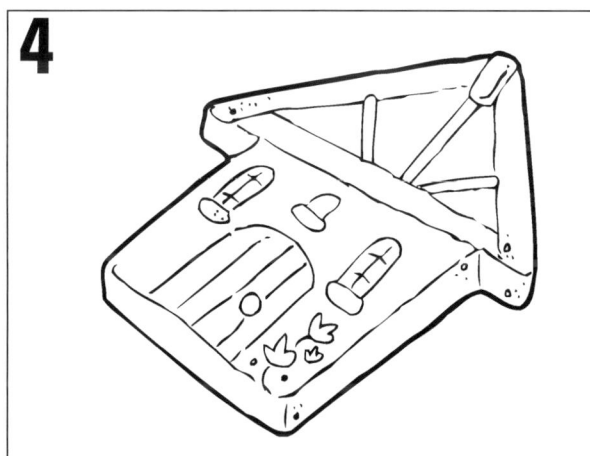

Use the utensils or excess clay to add detail to the house shape.

5

Poke a hole near the top to hang it.

6

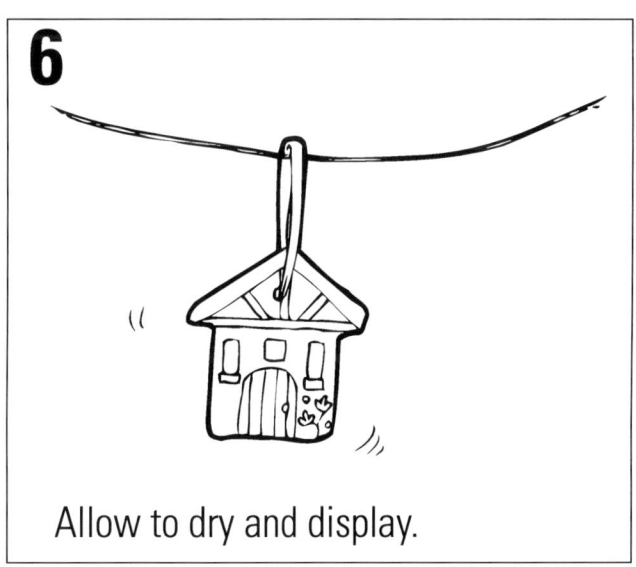

Allow to dry and display.

The multiple intelligence focus for this task is musical–rhythmic.

> A musical–rhythmic child has an awareness of music and sound.
> He/She learns best through activities involving music and rhythms.

Objective

- Writes community words in a musical form.

Preparation

- Children should be able to keep the beat to various songs or music using their body.
- Children should be involved in other musical activities such as group dances and percussion activities.

Teacher information

- A beat is a regular, constant rhythm such as a heartbeat or pulse.
- Encourage children to clap regular beats. No fast or slow beats should be included for this activity.
- Children may wish to learn the proper names of notes.
- A crotchet is worth one beat. ♩
- Other notes include the quaver (half a beat) ♪ , minim (two beats) ♩ and a semibreve ○, which is four beats.

Answers

1. (a) 1 (b) 2 (c) 4 (d) 4 (e) 2 (f) 4 (g) 2 (h) 5 (i) 2
2. Teacher check
3. Teacher check
4. Teacher check
5. Teacher check

Additional Activities

- Clap and keep the beat with songs about community helpers; for example 'The policeman's hat'.
- Match songs to an occupation; for example 'Sing a song of sixpence' may belong to someone who is a cook.
- Extend the activity by asking children to clap some words quickly; for example 'plumber' could be two quavers (two quick beats).

CURRICULUM LINKS		
England	Music	KS 1	• create musical patterns
Northern Ireland	Music	KS 1	• show awareness of pulse and rhythm
Republic of Ireland	Music	1st/ 2nd	• explore the natural speech rhythm of familiar words
Scotland	Music	A	• investigate sounds using voices and demonstrate some rhythm
Wales	Music	KS 1	• imitate short musical patterns

RHYTHMIC NAMES

You will write words in a musical form.

Task

1 Clap the words and write the number of beats in each word.

(a) *nurse* ☐   (b) *doctor* ☐   (c) *firefighter* ☐

(d) *librarian* ☐   (e) *dentist* ☐   (f) *electrician* ☐

(g) *plumber* ☐   (h) *police officer* ☐   (i) *chemist* ☐

2 In music, a ♩ is worth one beat. Draw the correct number of beats on the line next to each word.

(a) *nurse* _____   (b) *doctor* _____

(c) *firefighter* _____   (d) *librarian* _____

(e) *dentist* _____   (f) *electrician* _____

(g) *plumber* _____   (h) *police officer* _____

(i) *chemist* _____

3 Write your own name and clap it.

_____

How many beats does it have? ☐   Draw your name in beats. _____

4 Write and draw your teacher's name and two of your friends.

(a) *teacher* _____

(b) *friend 1* _____

(c) *friend 2* _____

5 Try this one! ***Doctor Knickerbocker.***

_____

www.prim-ed.com   105   Prim-Ed Publishing

MULTIPLE INTELLIGENCES

The multiple intelligence focus for this task is interpersonal.

An interpersonal child enjoys being in groups of teams.
He/She learns best through activities involving working with others.

Objective

- Works in a group to create a model of a community.

Preparation

- Various types of recycled materials should be collected to use for buildings etc.
- After planning, children may wish to collect particular materials from home to use. Time should be allowed for this.

Teacher information

- Children should form groups of four for this activity.
- Children may have more than one feature of a community to make. An extra sheet of paper will provide additional space for the answers to Question 3 if needed.
- Children should devise a simple plan for making a feature of a community. They need to collect appropriate materials to make the feature.
- After making the feature, children will place them together to form a community. Toys may be needed to complete the community scene.
- In this activity, it is just as important for the children to work well as a team as it is to make a good model.

Answers

Teacher check

Additional activities

- Children label all buildings, roads etc. on the model. Other groups may wish to view other models and compare their own. (visual–spatial)
- Groups discuss and give an evaluation of their design to the class, detailing any improvements which may be needed. (verbal–linguistic)

CURRICULUM LINKS			
England	Art & design	KS 1	• collaborate with others on projects in three dimensions
Northern Ireland	Art & design	KS 1	• make three dimensional structures by assembling, arranging and joining a variety of materials
Republic of Ireland	Visual arts	1st/ 2nd	• make imaginative structures
Scotland	Art & design	B	• create models and constructions from imagination and observation
Wales	Art	KS 1	• make objects in three dimensions using a range of materials

3-D COMMUNITY

people wise

1 List the members of your group.

2 Write the names of the buildings and features you wish to include in your model.

3 Decide who is going to make each feature and how he/she is going to make it.

(a) _____ will make _____ using

_____.

(b) _____ will make _____ using

_____.

(c) _____ will make _____ using

_____.

(d) _____ will make _____ using

_____.

4 Make the features for your community and display them. (Add toy cars, people and trees if you wish to!)

5 How well did your group work together?

very well	okay	not very well	awful

The multiple intelligence focus for this task is intrapersonal.

An intrapersonal child understands and analyses his/her thoughts and feelings.
He/She learns best through individual activities.

Objective

- Identifies problems in a community and offers solutions.

Preparation

- Children should have read the informational text on pages 92 and 93 before commencing this activity.

- Children should be aware of issues such as litter, graffiti, and vandalism.

Teacher information

- Discuss some problems in a community which children may have noticed. List these on the board.

- Discuss the correct words used to describe these problems; e.g. vandalism, litter, pollution.

- Children complete answers to Questions 1 to 4 independently.

- Worksheets may be shared with the remainder of the class. Discuss the problems identified.

Answers

- Teacher check

Additional activities

- Children collect articles from the local newspaper relating to community issues. (verbal–linguistic)

- Children create posters encouraging children to do the right thing to overcome these problems. For example, children may design posters to encourage others to pick up litter. (visual–spatial)

CURRICULUM LINKS			
England	PSHE	KS 1	• know what improves and harms their local environment and about some of the ways people look after them
Northern Ireland	Personal develop-ment*	KS 1	• know about conflict in their community, what is about and how they feel about it (* curriculum proposals)
Republic of Ireland	SPHE	1st/ 2nd	• appreciate the environment and realise that there is a community and individual responsibility for caring and protecting the environment
Scotland	PSD	B	• express views on values which are important to the community
Wales	PSE	KS 1	• understand how their environment could be made better to live in and how they can make a difference

COMMUNITY PROBLEMS

Task *You will identify a problem in a community and offer solutions.*

1 Draw a picture of a problem in your community.

2 Write about the problem. _____

_____

_____

3 List some solutions to the problem.

_____

_____

_____

_____

_____

4 How do you think you will be able to make your solution work? Will it be easy or hard?

_____

COMMUNITY – MY SELF-ASSESSMENT

After completing this unit, I was able to ...

word wise	use a familiar format to write information about a community.	☆ ☆ ☆ ☆ ☆
logic wise	conduct a survey to gather information about homes in the local community.	☆ ☆ ☆ ☆ ☆
nature wise	identify special places in the community and give reasons why they are special.	☆ ☆ ☆ ☆ ☆
picture wise	use a map of a community to find specific places.	☆ ☆ ☆ ☆ ☆
body wise	create a pottery house.	☆ ☆ ☆ ☆ ☆
music wise	write community words in a musical form.	☆ ☆ ☆ ☆ ☆
people wise	work in a group to create a model of a community.	☆ ☆ ☆ ☆ ☆
self wise	identify problems in a community and offer solutions.	☆ ☆ ☆ ☆ ☆

What I learnt

ME

Informational text ⸺ □ □ ⸺ Getting physical

All about me ⸺ □ □ ⸺ Body beat

Mad minute! ⸺ □ □ ⸺ Getting to know you

The five senses ⸺ □ □ ⸺ How do you feel?

Body jigsaw ⸺ □ □ ⸺ My self-assessment

What I know	What I want to know

Keywords

Name:	Date:

ME OVERVIEW

Verbal–Linguistic

- Ask children to write a list of things that make them special.
- Have children write about the most exciting thing that has happened to them.
- Write a diary about their daily life.
- Write a description about themselves.
- Write a newspaper article about something great they have done.
- Share a story about themselves or something that happened to them.
- Make up interview questions for a family survey about favourite things.
- Write an acrostic poem using the letters of their names.
- Write a description titled 'Me at 21'.
- Children bring treasured items to school and explain their importance to the class.
- Children write sentences about themselves; e.g. 'I am a good friend because ...', 'I like to eat ...'.

Logical–Mathematical

- Children calculate how many months until they finish primary school, how many weeks until their next birthday and so on.
- Children construct time lines that show some of the important events in their lives so far.
- Time how long it takes them to do certain activities; e.g. tie a shoelace.
- Calculate how old they are in years and months.
- Record the heights of class members. How many are taller than him/her? How many are shorter? What is the difference between him/her and the shortest/tallest child?
- Write their name in code. Can a partner work out the code?
- Draw a time line of the major events in their life so far.
- Measure and record their arm span, hand span, footstep, fingerprint, hair colour and so on.
- Compare and contrast their eyes, ears, noses and limbs with other animals such as an elephant, monkey or dog.
- Compare their physical attributes with those of other children.

Naturalist

- Have children write lists of physical facts about themselves. They can then discuss how they expect these to change as they grow older.
- Count heartbeats before and after exercise.
- Draw pictures to show how they have changed from birth to now.
- Give a talk about their favourite animal.
- Investigate their five senses.
- Discuss what children eat and how healthy individual diets are. Discuss or write ways to improve their diets.
- Learn about their body and how it works.
- Think about a beautiful outdoor place they'd like to be part of. Complete a chart using words to describe what it looks like, feels like and sounds like.

Visual–Spatial

- Children bring in photographs of themselves at different ages and write what has changed about themselves over time.
- Using a range of art materials, ask children to create their faces on paper plates. The materials provided may include wool, coloured paper, cotton wool.
- Paint or use textures to make a self-portrait.
- Label diagrams of the eye, ear and major organs.
- Make a mural which shows their favourite things to do, eat, places to go and so on.
- Trace around each child and have them paint or make a life-size collage of themselves.
- Children decorate their names in bold, bright patterns.
- Collect photos of children as babies to make a collage.
- Create self-portraits by using mirrors to view and record features to draw.
- Create a body jigsaw. Trace around a child lying on a sheet of paper. Cut into large pieces to make a jigsaw.
- Children show and talk about pictures and photos of themselves from birth to the present day.
- Children make puppets of themselves using recycled materials.
- Look at fingerprints and discuss the differences between individuals.
- Use 2-D shapes to construct a person.

ME OVERVIEW

Bodily–Kinaesthetic

- Children mime their reactions to different situations; e.g. finding out they have won a prize.
- Perform set movement patterns– running, hopping, climbing on or over or through equipment, rolling, sliding, galloping.
- Perform songs such as 'Hokey cokey'; ' Head, shoulders, knees and toes'.
- Make 3-D moulds of footprints and hand prints. Decorate with favourite things.
- Make up dance movements which focus on different body parts.
- Children role-play activities associated with feelings of personal happiness or unhappiness.
- Work in pairs to create mirror images of movement and expression.
- Discuss the importance of physical exercise. Does each child get enough exercise? How and why should they increase their fitness level?

- Show how they feel using facial and bodily expression; e.g. happy, sad, angry, sulky, frightened.
- Mime activities and hobbies they like to do for other children to guess.

Musical–Rhythmic

- Children stand in a circle. Each child can think of a rhythmic movement he/she can perform as he/she says the syllables of his her name. The class then repeats each name and movement.
- Listen to and share favourite songs with the class.
- Sing songs about 'me'; e.g. 'When you're happy and you know it'.
- Use musical instruments to copy syllable rhythms of children's names.
- Make musical patterns with instruments or body parts for others to copy.
- Create movement patterns in response to rhythm, music or words.
- Choose a song to clap the rhythm, then add some percussion.
- Write lyrics for a song about 'me', or a song that illustrates facts about 'me'.

Interpersonal

- Interview a classmate or friend to find out more about them.
- Sit in a circle–each child has a turn sitting in the middle while each child in the circle takes a turn to say one nice thing to or about the child in the middle.
- Work with a partner to find five things he/she has in common and five things that are uncommon.
- Find pictures in magazines or draw pictures to create a group chart about needs and wants.
- Teach a partner a skill he/she can do that the partner can't; e.g. handstand, threading a needle (and vice versa).
- Interview a partner about his/her likes/dislikes. The children can then compare these to their own.
- Video children in the class and playground. View the video while children explain the activities.
- Compile and discuss lists of rules children are expected to follow at school and home.

Intrapersonal

- Make a greeting card for themselves that describes what makes them special.
- Hold a 'Special talents day' for children to showcase sporting, artistic or musical talents.
- Ask children: 'If you could change one thing about yourself, what would it be and why?'
- Write a poem about themselves highlighting all their 'fantastic' features.
- Set to work towards achieving some personal goals.
- Write a journal of their lives over a one-week period.

- Compile lists of favourite things.
- Construct a family tree.
- Explore how they would feel given certain situations—e.g. being left out of a game—and what they could do about it.
- Research information about a personal hero.
- Create a family motto or coat of arms.
- Write a story about how they felt at a special time; e.g. first learning to ride a bike.

ME

INFORMATIONAL TEXT

We are all different

Everybody is unique. That means every person is different from another. We may seem alike in that we have eyes, ears, can move and laugh or cry. However, we are all different.

People are many DIFFERENT shapes and sizes.

They have DIFFERENT coloured hair, eyes and skin.

People like to do different things. No-one is exactly the same.

Everybody is good at something. Sometimes we need to keep practising things to get good at them. Some people are good at sport. Some people are good at music. Some people are good at lots of things! When we go to school, we get to try many things to find out what we are good at.

Our feelings are an important part of us. We can show others how we are feeling by the way we move our face and body. There are many different feelings such as happy, sad, angry, worried, scared or excited. When have you had these feelings?

The five senses

We learn about ourselves through using the five senses. These are seeing, hearing, smelling, tasting and touching. The sense organs are the eyes, ears, nose, tongue and skin. Nerve endings in these organs send information to our brain which then works out what is going on. For example, toast is burning. Nerve endings in your nose send a message to the brain which lets you know you can smell burnt toast.

Sight is the sense most often used, but we usually use more than one sense at a time. If someone does not have one of the senses he/she uses others to help them. For example, a person who cannot see can still 'read' books by using the sense of touch to read by Braille or the sense of hearing to listen to tapes or CDs.

ME

INFORMATIONAL TEXT

The skeleton

Did you know that a baby is born with about 350 bones? As the baby grows, many of these bones join together. An adult has 206 bones. All of our bones are known as our skeleton. It protects our body parts, allows us to stand upright and helps us to move.

The skull protects the brain.

The ribs protect the heart and lungs.

The bones have joints which allow the skeleton to bend.

Organs of the body

We have talked about the sense organs earlier. Other important organs are shown in the picture below.

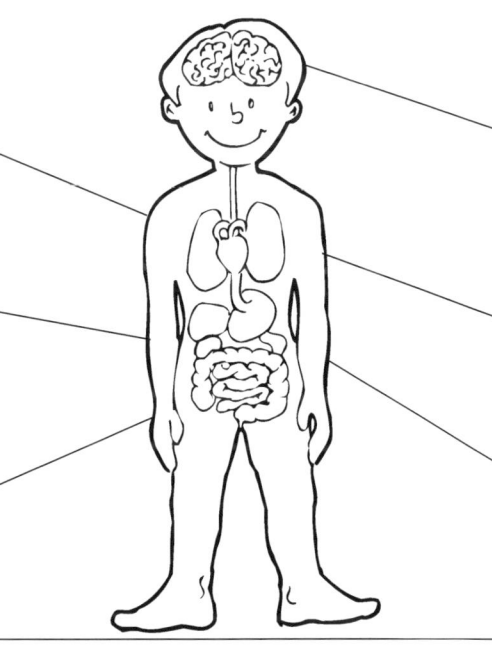

The **heart** pumps blood containing oxygen all around our body.

The **kidneys** help get rid of wastes.

The **intestines** carry wastes out of the body.

The **brain** controls our feeling, thinking and movement.

Our **lungs** fill up with air when we breathe in.

The **stomach** digests food. The **liver** also helps us to digest food.

Keeping healthy

There are lots of things we should do to keep our body healthy. We need to eat healthy food, get plenty of sleep, drink lots of water, make time to relax, keep our bodies clean, visit the dentist and doctor and do some exercise.

Different types of exercise can be lots of fun. Some people play sports, dance, swim or walk. When we exercise we may feel warmer, sweaty, breathe faster, have a faster heartbeat, feel thirsty, get a red face or feel tired. Keeping fit can also make us feel happier, healthier and full of energy.

The multiple intelligence focus for this activity is verbal–linguistic.

> A verbal–linguistic child thinks in words.
> He/She learns best through activities involving reading, writing and speaking.

Objectives

- Writes and constructs a booklet about himself/herself to share with others.
- Identifies features of his/her physical appearance.
- Identifies and appreciates positive personal qualities.

Preparation

- Children will need scissors to cut out the booklet, which would be better enlarged to A3.
- Thumbprints can be made with coloured paint. Children will need to practise making prints to work out the correct amount of paint before impressing on their booklet.

Teacher information

- Before children complete the booklet individually, discuss each section and the vocabulary that might be needed.
- The photograph space on the cover page is for children to glue a photo or draw a picture of their face only.
- For page 2, children will need to practise making thumbprints as outlined above. Discuss and write on the board hair and eye colours (e.g. hazel, blond, brunette), hairstyles (e.g. spiky, curly, short) and complexions (e.g. olive, freckled, pale). Children will also need to be measured and weighed.
- For page 3, children think of a category of their own for the blank box.
- When the booklet is completed, children can read their books to a partner or small group or swap with others to read.

Answers

- Teacher check

Additional activities

- Use some of the categories in the book to graph characteristics such as children's eye or hair colour, favourite hobby or food. Use pictograms or bar graphs. (logical–mathematical)
- Discuss the similarities and differences among the physical characteristics children identified. Do the same with the positive personal qualities. (This could relate to a tolerance theme in health and values.) (interpersonal)

CURRICULUM LINKS			
England	English	KS 1	• assemble information from own experience and use language and features of non-fiction texts to make class books
Northern Ireland	English	KS 1	• write for a variety of purposes, including to describe and report
Republic of Ireland	English	1st/ 2nd	• write in a variety of genres
Scotland	English	B	• use different forms of functional writing
Wales	English	KS 1	• write in a range of forms

ALL ABOUT ME

Task *You will write and make a booklet about yourself to share with others.*

word wise

These are my favourite things.

People	Foods
Sport/Hobby	TV show
	Pet/Animal

Eye colour

Hair colour

Thumbprint

Hair style

Complexion

Weight   Height

cm   kg

I'm a star!

The thing I do best ...

My best quality ...

A good deed I've done ...

My proudest moment ...

All about me!

Name

Address

Phone

Birthday

The multiple intelligence focus for this activity is logical–mathematical.

> A logical–mathematical child thinks rationally and in abstractions.
> He/She learns best through activities involving problem-solving, numbers and patterns.

Objectives

- Estimates and then counts the number of times he/she can do an activity in one minute.

- Practises each activity to improve the number of repetitions in a minute.

Preparation

- Stopwatches, clocks/watches with second hands, or timers will be needed.

- Ensure children know how to use these devices.

- Collect equipment for the activities—paper, skipping ropes, tennis balls, basketballs, scissors, zip-up pencil cases, coloured pencils, beanbags, washing baskets and blocks.

- The activities will need both indoor and outdoor areas.

Teacher information

- Children should practise estimating the duration of one minute to assist them in working out the amount of repetitions for each activity.

- Children could work in groups of three. One child times, one child completes the activity and the other child assists in counting repetitions.

- Discuss other activities to write for numbers 11 and 12.

- Discuss and demonstrate acceptable executions for each activity; e.g. activity 1- the names must be clear enough to read, activity 3 the ball must be thrown above the head (children will learn not to throw it too high or it will take too long). Unsuccessful executions should not be counted.

- This activity should be continued over a few sessions. Allow time to practise during class time—many children will practise some activities during breaks and at home!

- Children should work out why or why not they improved with each attempt.

Answers

- Teacher check

Additional activities

- Choose one activity and graph his/her own and four other classmates' best results.

- Compare and contrast other classmates' results.

- Extend the activity to one and half minutes or two minutes. Did repetitions double at two minutes? Why/Why not?

CURRICULUM LINKS			
England	Numeracy	Yr 1/2	• use vocabulary related to time and use units of time
Northern Ireland	Maths	KS 1	• use mathematical language associated with time and use units to measure in purposeful contexts
Republic of Ireland	Maths	1st/ 2nd	• use vocabulary of time
Scotland	Maths	A	• complete time activities
Wales	Maths	KS 1	• use appropriate language of time and standard units of time

MAD MINUTE!

Task — *You will guess and count the number of times you can do an activity in one minute.*

1 (a) Read each activity below. Add two of your own. Make a guess about how many you think you will do in one minute. Now try each one and write the answer.

(b) Practise doing each activity, then see if you improve each time.

	Activity	Guess	Number in one minute			Did you improve? ✓ or ✗
			1st try	2nd try	3rd try	
1	Write your first name and surname.					
2	Jump with a skipping rope.					
3	Throw a tennis ball above your head and catch it.					
4	Sit down on the floor and stand up while your hands are on your head.					
5	Bounce a basketball with one hand only.					
6	Cut out rectangles from scrap paper.					
7	Count backwards by fives from 50 to 5.					
8	Throw a beanbag into a washing basket two metres away.					
9	Balance six blocks on top of each other.					
10	Pack six coloured pencils into a zip-up pencil case and close the zip. Take them out and repeat.					
11						
12						

The multiple intelligence focus for this activity is naturalist.

> A naturalist child has an awareness of the patterns in nature.
> He/She learns best through activities involving animals, plants and the environment.

Objectives

- Uses his/her five senses to make observations with each receptor organ.
- Completes a cloze about the five senses.

Preparation

- Collect and prepare items for Questions 2 (d) and (e)—slices of lemon, crisps, jam, cotton wool, water and sticks or twigs.
- Saucers, teaspoons and small cups will be needed to display items.

Teacher information

- Children may need to refer to the informational text on page 114 to complete the cloze.
- In Questions 2 (d) and (e) children will need to taste and touch the items listed to complete the activity accurately and not just rely on memory or 'common' sense!

  Caution: Be aware of any child allergies, or other food-related health problems.

Answers

(Refer to informational text on page 114.)

1. 1. ourselves

    2. five   3. seeing

    4. tasting   5. ears

    6. skin   7. Sight

    8. see   9. books

2. Teacher check

Additional activities

- Discuss how people manage when one or more of their senses is partially or totally impaired; e.g. eyesight – glasses, use of Braille; hearing – hearing aid, sign language; sense of smell and taste are often reduced when you have a cold.

- Play a guessing game with the senses. An object is placed in a box. Children first listen to guess the object (shake box etc.) and write an answer. They use the following senses in order – smell and touch (using **only** that sense) and guess the object each time. (Explain that taste will not be used as it is unhygienic.) Finally, sight is used to check the correct answer.

CURRICULUM LINKS			
England	Science	KS 1	• know humans use their senses to be aware of the world around them
Northern Ireland	Science	KS 1	• find out about themselves, including how to use their senses
Republic of Ireland	Science	1st/ 2nd	• become aware of the role of each sense in detecting information about the environment
Scotland	Science	B	• give examples of how the senses are used to detect information
Wales	Science	KS 1	• know humans have and use senses which enable them to be aware of the world around them

THE FIVE SENSES

Task *You will use your five senses to make observations with your eyes, ears, nose, tongue and skin.*

1 Use the information on page 114 to complete the paragraph below about your senses.

We learn about _____ (1) through using the _____ (2)

senses. These are _____ (3), hearing, smelling, _____ (4)

and touching. The sense organs are the eyes, _____ (5), nose, tongue and

_____ (6). _____ (7) is the sense most often used, but we

usually use more than one sense at a time. If someone does not have one of the

senses, he/she uses others to help. For example, a person who cannot

_____ (8) can still 'read' _____ (9) by listening to tapes or using Braille.

2 Use each of your senses to complete the activities below.

(a) Draw two things in the classroom that end in 't'.

(b) List two smells you like and two you don't like.

Like ....

Don't like ....

(c) List two sounds you can hear in the room and two you can hear outside the room.

In ....

Out ....

(d) Write 'sweet', 'salty' or 'sour' next to each food.

lemon ....

jam ....

crisps ....

(e) Use one or two words to describe how these things feel.

cotton wool ....

stick ....

water ....

The multiple intelligence focus for this activity is visual–spatial.

> A visual–spatial child thinks in images, colours and shape.
> He/She learns best through activities involving visualisation.

Objectives

- Assembles a jigsaw of a human body.
- Identifies and labels major parts of the human body.

Preparation

- Find a chart, picture or model of the human body.

Teacher information

- Use the chart or model to show the different parts of the human body.
- Name and label the names of specific external parts of the human body.
- Discuss what each of the body parts can do.
- Children cut out the body parts on the worksheet and assemble the jigsaw on the outline.
- Ask children to orally give the answers to the labelling activity (Question 2) as a class. Note: This is a learning activity not a test, so sharing information is important. On the board, write the correct spelling of the body parts for children to refer to.

Answers

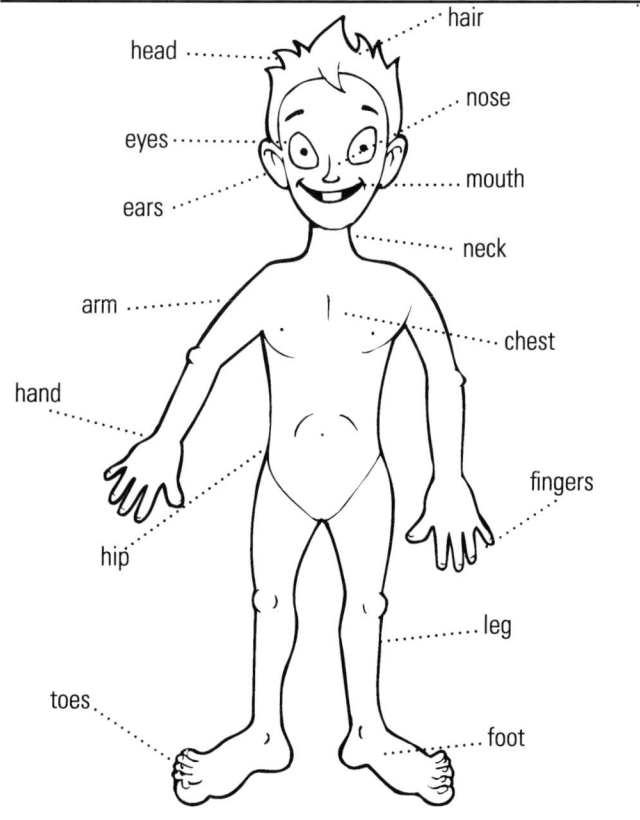

Additional activities

- Make body 'mobiles' using paper strips and split pins. Label body parts.
- Look at diagrams of the bodies of animals. How are they similar or different to the human body?
- Read and discuss the book *The magic schoolbus in the human body* by Joanna Cole and Bruce Degan. (verbal–linguistic)
- Sing action songs which use body parts, e.g. *Head, shoulders, knees and toes*. (musical–rhythmic)

CURRICULUM LINKS			
England	Science	KS 1	• recognise the main external parts of the bodies of humans
Northern Ireland	Science	KS 1	• recognise and name the main external parts of the human body
Republic of Ireland	Science	1st/ 2nd	• name and identify external parts of the body
Scotland	Science	A	• name and identify the main external parts of the bodies of humans
Wales	Science	KS 1	• name the main external parts of the human body

BODY JIGSAW

picture wise

1 (a) Cut out the body parts below and glue them onto the body outline.

(b) Finish the labels on the body.

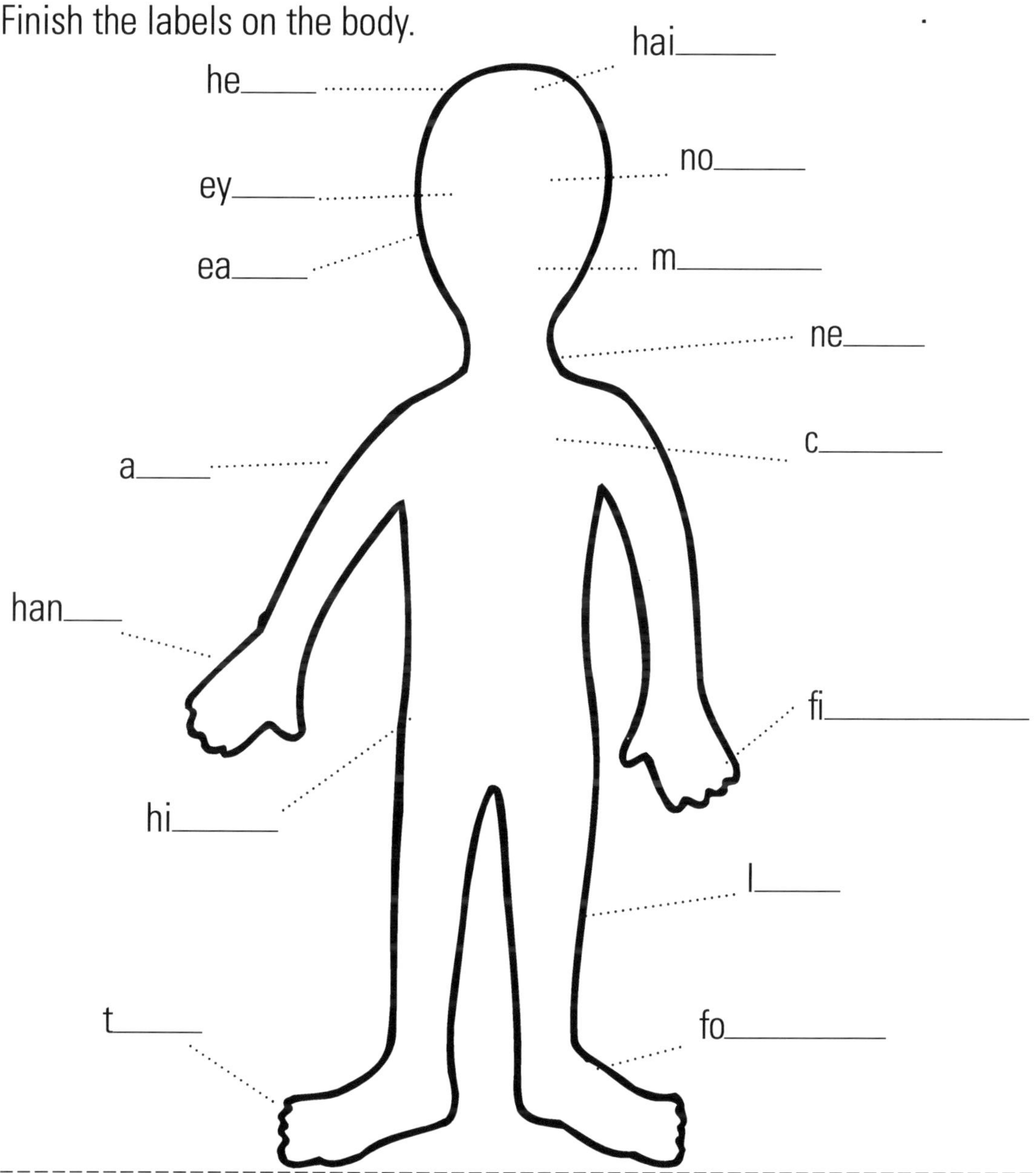

hai_____

he_____

no_____

ey_____

ea_____

m_____

ne_____

a_____

c_____

han_____

fi_____

hi_____

l_____

t_____

fo_____

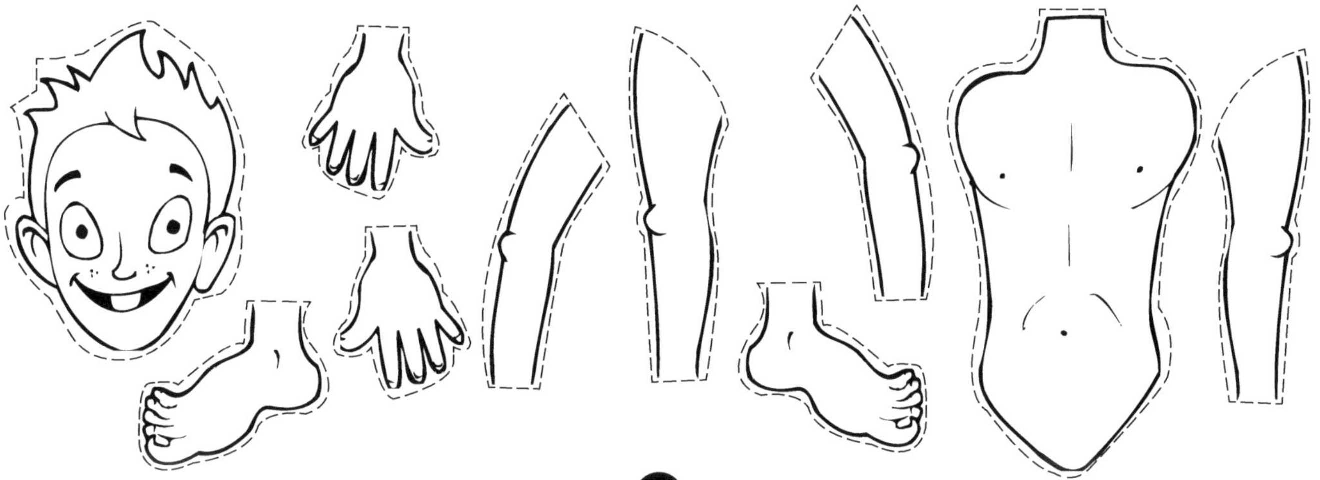

The multiple intelligence focus for this activity is bodily–kinaesthetic.

A bodily–kinaesthetic child has good physical awareness.
He/She learns best through 'hands-on' activities.

Objectives

- Recognises the effects of exercise on the body.
- Identifies sporting activities he/she is involved in.

Preparation

- Discussion points
  - Why do you exercise?
  - How does exercise make your body feel?
  - What types of exercise do you do?
  - How do you feel before, during and after physical activity?
  - Why do you feel this way?
  - How does your body change after exercise?
  - What is the best thing about your favourite sport?

Teacher information

- During physical activity, the body undergoes immediate changes. These include changes in body temperature, perspiration, heart rate and breathing rate. Participants may feel thirsty, hot, sweaty and fatigued.

- Physical activity can help with weight control, a healthier heart, improved lung capacity, clearer skin, good muscle tone, better sleep patterns and more energy. It can also provide teamwork skills, discipline, commitment, improved self-esteem and confidence.

Answers

1. Answers will vary
2. Possible answers 'feel warmer', 'my heart beats faster', 'I perspire more', 'I puff more', 'my breathing is faster', 'I feel thirsty'.
3. Answers will vary

Additional activities

- Children can write an account of their favourite sport and present it to the class or in small groups as an oral speaking activity (verbal–linguistic)

- Children can graph the results of how much time they spend exercising and what types of exercise they do.

- Children draw or collect pictures of their favourite sportspeople to make a class collage. (visual–spatial)

CURRICULUM LINKS			
England	PE	KS 1	• know it is important to be active and recognise and describe how their bodies feel during different activities
Northern Ireland	PE	KS 1	• be aware of the relationship between exercise and physical well-being and recognise the effects of activity on the body, including sweating, faster heart beat and being out of breath
Republic of Ireland	SPHE	1st/ 2nd	• appreciate the need and understand how to care for the body in order to keep it strong and healthy, e.g. regular exercise
Scotland	PE	B	• know and describe some of the obvious effects of exercise on the body
Wales	PSE	KS 1	• know that exercise is important to keep their bodies healthy

GETTING PHYSICAL

body wise

1 Colour the boxes to show some of the types of exercise you do.

red= every day   *blue* = most days   *green* = some days   *orange* = hardly ever

☐ .... walk to school

☐ ...... walk with family/friends

☐ .... play at lunchtime

☐ .... play a sport after school

☐ .... PE at school

☐ .... ride my bike

☐ .... play a sport at school

☐ .....play in the park after school

2 Colour the boxes.

When I exercise:		
I feel warmer	I perspire more	my breathing is faster
I feel cooler	I perspire less	my breathing is slower
my heart beats faster	I puff more	I feel thirsty
my heartbeat slows down	I puff less	I do not feel thirsty

3 (a) Draw a picture of you playing your favourite sport.

(b) Why do you like to play this sport?

_____

_____

_____

(c) Where do you play this sport?

_____

(d) How do you feel after playing this sport? Tick the best boxes.

☐ healthy   ☐ full of energy

☐ tired   ☐ fit

☐ happy   ☐ lazy

The multiple intelligence focus for this activity is musical–rhythmic.

> A musical–rhythmic child has an awareness of music and sound.
> He/She learns best through activities involving music or rhythms.

Objectives

- Identifies and records sounds using different body parts to create simple rhythm.
- Works with a group to create and perform simple rhythms.

Preparation

- View and listen to a variety of music or videos where body sounds play a part (e.g. foot stomping, finger clicking).
- Ensure children have a safe environment to move, record and perform.
- Emphasis is on 'musical' body sounds and not those that may cause harm.
- Preselect working groups. Allow groups time for sharing ideas, planning, preparation and practice of their musical piece.
- Ensure children are proficient at keeping a rhythmic beat using percussion instruments or body percussion.
- Children should have viewed, listened to or learnt a number of ways with body percussion before commencing this activity.
- Children should work in small groups (3–5) to share, plan, create practise and perform their 'body beat' rhythm.

Teacher information

- Body percussion involves creating a beat using various parts of the body, such as clapping, clicking fingers, stamping, creating sounds using the mouth and hands etc.
- A rhythm is a regular arrangement of sound that forms a continuing pattern. Encourage children to repeat body sounds—for example, three clicks, two stomps, five slaps—to make interesting rhythmic patterns.
- Allow children to experiment and record ideas individually before moving into a group.
- Groups can listen to the rhythms of individuals and then plan a group rhythm to present to the class using body percussion.
- Groups may like to choose original rhythms created by individuals or the group or use body percussion to perform a known tune (e.g. 'Three blind mice').

Answers

- Teacher check

Additional activities

- Teach simple 'me' songs to the class. Check out this website for 'me' songs sung to known tunes like 'Three blind mice'.

  http://www.preschooleducation.com/sme.shtml

- Make simple percussion instruments to use for a variety of musical accompaniments; for example, rice maracas, water bottle xylophone, bottle top tambourine. (bodily–kinaesthetic)

- Use water-based paints to paint character faces on a partner's knees. Select music to make these characters 'move' or 'dance'. (bodily–kinaesthetic)

CURRICULUM LINKS			
England	Music	KS 1	• create musical patterns using sounds made in different ways
Northern Ireland	Music	KS 1	• explore and investigate ways of making sounds
Republic of Ireland	Music	1st/ 2nd	• discover ways of making sounds using body percussion
Scotland	Music	A	• explore sounds they can make with their voices or bodies
Wales	Music	KS 1	• improvise, compose and arrange music using a variety of sound sources, e.g. their bodies

BODY BEAT

You will write about and test different body parts to make sounds and simple rhythms.

music wise

1 What sounds/actions can you make with your …

… hands?

… feet?

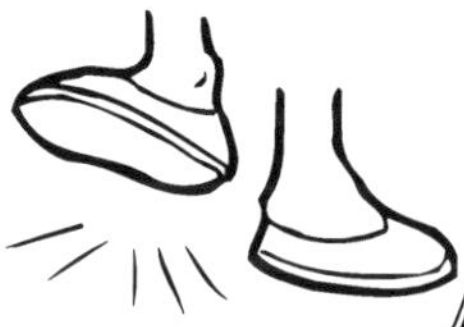

… tongue?

… fingers?

… mouth?

Circle three favourite sounds.

Use these sounds to make a fun rhyme.

Share your rhyme with a partner.

How does it sound?

2 Which sounds would you use for …

your name?
your best friend's name?

1 2 3 4 5

The multiple intelligence focus for this activity is interpersonal.

An interpersonal child enjoys being in groups or teams.
He/She learns best through activities involving working with others.

Objective

- Conducts an interview with a partner and records his/her responses.

Preparation

- Divide the class into pairs.
- Each child must take a turn at being the interviewer and the interviewee.
- Discuss the purpose of an interview and the roles of the participants.

Teacher information

- An interview involves the meeting of at least two people: an interviewer and an interviewee. The interviewer asks questions in order to gain information from and discuss ideas with the interviewee. The interviewer's purpose is to draw out special information so that he/she (or others) is more informed.
- Allow children time to swap roles and discuss recorded results.
- At the end of the session, ask pairs to orally share something new or interesting they have found out about their partner to the class.

Answers

Teacher check

Additional activities

- Design a 'me' badge. Draw pictures (3–4) to show things that best represent them (e.g. names, initials, things he/she is good at, things he/she likes). (visual–spatial)
- Send home a plain paper grocery bag for children to decorate with things about themselves. (e.g. family, favourite things). Inside the bag, children can place one favourite toy. Each child talks to the class about the inside/outside of his/her bag. (verbal–linguistic)
- Make a personal ID kit consisting of fingerprints, lip prints, baby photograph, current photograph and other important details. (visual–spatial)

CURRICULUM LINKS			
England	English	KS 1	• speak to different people and listen to each other
Northern Ireland	English	KS 1	• work in pairs and ask and answer questions
Republic of Ireland	English	1st/ 2nd	• engage in real situations involving language use
Scotland	English	A/B	• talk to peers, making notes as they listen
Wales	English	KS 1	• talk for a range of purposes and listen carefully

GETTING TO KNOW YOU

people wise

What is your full name?	When is your birthday?
What is your favourite … colour? _____ food? _____ TV show? _____ song? _____ book? _____ sport? _____	Who are the people in your family?
	What are you really good at?
	What was your proudest moment?
What jobs do you do at home?	What makes you happy?
Who are your closest friends?	What would you really like to do when you grow up?

The multiple intelligence focus for this activity is intrapersonal.

An intrapersonal child understands and analyses his/her thoughts and feelings.
He/She learns best through individual activities.

Objective

- Identifies feelings to match a situation.

Teacher information

- Different situations evoke different emotions. Children should be aware that each of us reacts to different situations in different ways. Body language, such as facial expressions, stance and body position, is a key to how a person is feeling. Children need to learn to show feelings in ways that are helpful to them and others and not in ways that are hurtful.

- Brainstorm 'feeling' words with children. Work in pairs to express each emotion (e.g. excited, sad, scared, angry, worried, happy)

- Discuss situations when children may experience each emotion.

  – Which situations do children have different feelings about? (e.g. a birthday—happy, excited)

  – Which situations do children feel the same about? (e.g. happy times, sad times)

  – Which feelings are good? (positive)

  – Which feelings are bad? (negative)

- Discuss scenes in Question 1 (being hurt by others, being with friends, running late for class).

Answers

- Teacher check

Additional activities

- Practise using facial expressions, stance and body position to show anger, sadness, shyness, happiness, excitement, worry etc. Mime them for others to guess the feelings you are showing. (bodily–kinaesthetic)

- View and discuss feelings and facial expressions of characters in shared reading books. (verbal–linguistic)

- In groups, children make a poster of how to react when feeling angry. Add drawings or magazine pictures to the posters. (interpersonal)

CURRICULUM LINKS			
England	PSHE	KS 1	• recognise, name and deal with feelings
Northern Ireland	Personal develop-ment*	KS 1	• recognise their own feelings (* proposed curriculum)
Republic of Ireland	SPHE	1st/ 2nd	• name and identify a wide range of feelings and talk about and explore feelings in different situations
Scotland	PSD		• recognise feelings
Wales	PSE	KS 1	• be aware of their own feelings and begin to understand the range of feelings in different situations

HOW DO YOU FEEL?

self wise

1 Look at the pictures. Colour the face which shows how you would feel if this was happening to you.

2 Draw a face or write about how you feel.

(a) You are going to a friend's birthday.	(b) Someone pinched you.
(c) You fell off your bike.	(d) Your team won.
(e) You dropped your dinner plate.	(f) You are lost in a crowd.

3 When do you feel ...

happy?	excited?	angry?

ME – MY SELF-ASSESSMENT

After completing this unit, I was able to ...

word wise	write and make a booklet about myself to share with others.	☆ ☆ ☆ ☆ ☆
logic wise	guess and count the number of times I did an activity in one minute.	☆ ☆ ☆ ☆ ☆
nature wise	use my sense organs to make observations.	☆ ☆ ☆ ☆ ☆
picture wise	complete a jigsaw of the body and label the body parts.	☆ ☆ ☆ ☆ ☆
body wise	write about my favourite sport and understand the importance of exercise.	☆ ☆ ☆ ☆ ☆
music wise	write about and use different body parts to make sounds and simple rhythms.	☆ ☆ ☆ ☆ ☆
people wise	interview a partner and record his/her answers.	☆ ☆ ☆ ☆ ☆
self wise	draw or write about different feelings.	☆ ☆ ☆ ☆ ☆

What I learnt